THE OTHER SIDE OF THE COIN

The Other Side of the Coin

PUBLIC OPINION TOWARD SOCIAL TAX EXPENDITURES

Christopher Ellis and Christopher Faricy

Russell Sage Foundation   NEW YORK

LIBRARY OF CONGRESS CATALOGING-IN-PUBLICATION DATA

Names: Ellis, Christopher, 1978- author. | Faricy, Christopher G., 1973- author.
Title: The other side of the coin : public opinion toward social tax expenditures / Christopher Ellis, Christopher Faricy.
Description: New York : Russell Sage Foundation, [2021] | Includes bibliographical references and index. | Summary: "The United States provides economic security to citizens through a divided welfare state—one in which citizens receive benefits through both direct public programs and indirect tax subsidies. Studies of public opinion toward social policy have focused almost exclusively on direct programs; the purpose of this book is to understand public opinion toward tax expenditure programs—the "other side" of the American social welfare state. It examines how citizens form attitudes toward social tax expenditures, which not only are central to American economic security but also represent a significant portion of the federal budget, and how the design of social tax expenditure programs structure opinions toward social spending. The authors explore how social tax expenditures are expanding into new areas and might provide a way to expand the federal government's role in addressing the social problems caused by rising inequality and growing economic dislocation while doing so in a way that is palatable to a public that is generally skeptical and distrusting of government"—Provided by publisher.
Identifiers: LCCN 2020037284 (print) | LCCN 2020037285 (ebook) | ISBN 9780871544407 (paperback) | ISBN 9781610449045 (ebook)
Subjects: LCSH: Federal aid to public welfare—United States. | Tax expenditures—United States. | Economic assistance, Domestic—United States.
Classification: LCC HV95 .E54 2020 (print) | LCC HV95 (ebook) | DDC 361.6/10973—dc23
LC record available at https://lccn.loc.gov/2020037284
LC ebook record available at https://lccn.loc.gov/2020037285

Text design by Linda Secondari.

RUSSELL SAGE FOUNDATION
112 East 64th Street, New York, NY 10065
10 9 8 7 6 5 4 3 2 1

To my loving family—Lauren, Nathan, and Mitchell
To Connor, Charlotte, and Carrie, for your patience and love

CONTENTS

ILLUSTRATIONS

Figures

Tables

ABOUT THE AUTHORS

CHRISTOPHER ELLIS is professor of political science at Bucknell University.

CHRISTOPHER FARICY is associate professor of political science at Syracuse University.

ACKNOWLEDGMENTS

CHRIS FARICY would like to thank colleagues at Syracuse University for offering insightful feedback on selected chapters from this book. Shana Gadarian, Seth Jolly, and Dan McDowell offered valued comments on various parts of this book. Spencer Piston was an early supporter of our project and offered important critiques on the work. Brandon Metroka, Joel Kersting, and Nicholas Croce were invaluable research assistants who helped gather data and prior studies as well as offered edits on the manuscript. I would also like to thank Christine Leigh Docteur and Caroline McMullin for their excellent advice and support on our grant application to the Russell Sage Foundation. Finally, I would like to thank Grant Reeher and the Campbell Public Affairs Institute for their financial support.

Chris Ellis would like to thank Amy Wolaver and the Bucknell Institute for Public Policy for generously donating survey time though their Survey Research Laboratory over the period of several years. Their in-kind support allowed us to conduct many of the surveys and analyses in this book. I would also like to thank Joe Ura, Scott Meinke, John Doces, and members of the Bucknell Political Science Department for conversations that helped to improve the final manuscript.

Together, we would like to thank the following for all of the support and guidance we have received from the Russell Sage Foundation. James Wilson, Nora Mitnick, and Irina Lotarevich were very helpful in navigating the logistics around our RSF grant. We would like to thank the anonymous reviewers who provided particularly important advice on

organizing the sections in the book and giving more shape to the theoretical argument. We would also like to thank Marcelo Agudo for the
improvements made to the manuscript through the copyediting process.
We are principally thankful for Suzanne Nichols's sage advice and expert
guidance through the book publishing process. Suzanne offered timely
suggestions for our manuscript and title and showed amazing patience
with our pace of writing.

CHAPTER 1

Public Opinion Toward the Hidden Welfare State

AMERICAN FAMILIES are living through a new Gilded Age of increasingly high levels of income inequality, decades of wage stagnation, and widespread economic anxiety.[1] In 2019, despite a decade of economic growth and historically low levels of unemployment, income inequality in the United States as measured by the Gini coefficient reached its highest level.[2] In comparison to other democratic nations, the U.S. government has taken few direct steps to remedy this growing inequality, at least in part because of public opinion, which is a highly influential factor in determining the size and scope of the American welfare state.[3] Despite evidence of growing public concern about inequality, public support for direct government solutions to income equality and declining economic opportunity has by some accounts dropped in recent years.[4] However, while direct social welfare programs have not been drastically expanded, there has been growth in social tax expenditure programs that help citizens pay for expenses such as health insurance, the rising costs of college, and investments in retirement plans. The purpose of this book is to understand public opinion toward tax expenditure programs—the "other side" of the American social welfare state.

The United States provides economic security to citizens through a divided welfare state in which citizens receive benefits through both direct public programs and indirect tax subsidies.[5] As an example, the United States offers people health care insurance not only through Medicare and

Medicaid but also through subsidies for employer-provided health care insurance, which is used by the majority of working adults. The federal government assists workers in obtaining retirement security not just with Social Security but also through the various tax subsidies for 401(k) and IRA plans. And although the poor are aided through direct programs such as welfare and food stamps, the largest federal antipoverty program is the Earned Income Tax Credit (EITC). Studies of public opinion toward social policy have focused almost exclusively on direct spending programs such as Medicare and welfare. In this book, we set out to thoroughly examine how citizens form attitudes toward social tax expenditures and how the design of social tax expenditure programs structure opinions toward social spending.

Social Tax Expenditures for Private Welfare

Social policy is any government program that provides economic security by protecting against income loss and providing a minimum standard of living. So our study of public opinion toward social policy in America not only looks at attitudes toward public programs but also considers attitudes toward federal tax subsidies for the private provision of social benefits and services. A tax expenditure is a special provision in the federal tax code, such as an exclusion, deduction, exemption, or credit, that is used to finance groups of citizens or designated activities. The government, in other words, can choose to finance social benefits either through direct spending, by writing checks to citizens or otherwise directly covering the cost of those benefits, or through tax expenditures, which allow citizens who use government-approved private social services to write smaller checks to the federal government.

Budget experts argue that targeted tax breaks for social welfare should be considered "expenditures" since this policy tool shares many characteristics with direct spending. A tax expenditure is, after all, a government-directed allocation of money to specific populations or activities that in turn has an economic effect on the market, the consumer, and the federal budget.[6] Formally, the federal government generates annual tax expenditure estimates that allow for a side-by-side comparison of programs funded through the tax code and those funded through the appropriations process.[7] And while some social tax expenditures are used to make public social benefits

Table 1.1 Americans' Use of Major Social Tax Expenditure Programs, 2015

Tax Status	Percentage
Enrolled in employer-provided health insurance	49.9%
Paying home mortgage interest	42.9
Enrolled in employer retirement plan/401(k)	39.6

Source: Estimates from YouGov survey, August 2015.

such as Social Security tax-free, the vast majority of these programs are used to subsidize the supply of private-sector social insurance and benefits. Therefore, the federal government finances both the public and private sides of the divided welfare state in America.

It is important to study public opinion toward social tax expenditures because the major social tax expenditure programs assist wide swaths of the American public, including homeowners, employees with employment-based health care insurance, workers who invest in 401(k)s and IRAs, households with student loan debt, parents with children in college, parents saving for college, households with large medical expenses, low-income workers, and families with young children, to name a few. Table 1.1 presents survey data from YouGov of a nationally representative survey of one thousand respondents in 2015 showing the importance of a handful of major social tax expenditures to the average household's safety net. One out of two respondents relied on the largest program in the tax code: employment-based health insurance coverage and the accompanying federal tax subsidies, which alone cost the federal government $172.8 billion in 2019. There are also tax expenditures covering health insurance for the self-employed and programs to help employers and employees purchase insurance through the health care markets created by the Patient Protection and Affordable Care Act (ACA) of 2010.

Investments and savings constitute another part of an average household's economic security plan. There are a number of federal subsidies for private pensions, such as tax expenditures for defined-benefit programs, defined-contribution programs, and Roth IRAs. The main vehicle for workers to gain access to the stock market is through their employer-provided retirement plans such as 401(k)s or IRAs. We found in our survey that around 40 percent of U.S. adults are enrolled in some type of employer-sponsored retirement plan. The federal tax code also

Figure 1.1 Federal Spending, Including Social Tax Expenditures, 2016

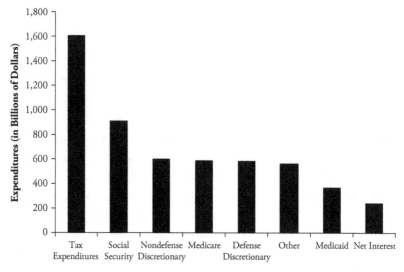

Source: Joint Committee on Taxation data, available at: https://www.jct.gov/publications.html?func=select&id=6 (accessed September 24, 2020), and Congressional Budget Office 2016.

encourages Americans to save for social welfare–related expenses, including medical payments, higher education costs, and unemployment. According to U.S. census data, roughly 60 percent of American households own homes, and around 40 percent of American households are making mortgage payments. These homeowners can benefit from social tax expenditure programs that allow them to deduct the interest on their home mortgages and the property taxes that they pay to state and local governments. In the past, American families have tapped their increasingly valuable homes and retirement accounts for emergency funds during times of economic crisis.[8] In short, social tax expenditures are not ancillary programs; for most American families they are in fact the main form of federal financial assistance supporting their economic security.

Not only are social tax expenditures central to Americans' economic security, but they also represent a significant portion of the federal budget. The Congressional Budget Office (CBO) estimated the 2016 formal budget at $3.9 trillion.[9] In that same year, the federal government spent $1.6 trillion on tax expenditure programs. Figure 1.1 shows how tax expenditures compare to traditional budgetary spending categories. In 2016, the overall tax expenditure budget, at $1.6 trillion, was larger than Social Security and Medicare combined ($1.5 trillion) and more than total discretionary spending ($1.18 trillion). In some policy areas, such as housing, the federal government spends more on tax subsidies than on direct budgetary payments. In 2016, $171.4 billion was spent on just four private pension subsidy plans, and $155.3 billion was allocated to just one health insurance program for employment-based plans. These are not small or minor federal programs. And in more and more social policy areas, the ratio of federal spending is shifting away from budgetary spending and toward tax expenditures.

Yet, despite the importance of social tax expenditures to both the federal budget and Americans' economic security, there has been little systematic study of public attitudes toward these types of federal social programs.[10] And these few studies pale in comparison to the abundance of studies on public opinion toward public social welfare programs such as Social Security and welfare. We are left with an asymmetric understanding of the role of public opinion in the divided welfare state: while public opinion is an established influence on changes to public social spending, it is understudied on the private side.

Tax expenditures for social welfare are commonly referred to as the "hidden" or "submerged" welfare state in American politics, in the sense that they are an off-budget subsidy used to finance private providers rather than a program that is part of the formal budget and provides direct assistance to citizens, such as Social Security.[11] There are other characteristics that separate a tax expenditure from a direct public spending program. A tax expenditure program is passed on the revenue side of the budget process, controlled by just a few congressional committees, and administered by the Internal Revenue Service (IRS). The exclusive jurisdiction over these programs given to the congressional tax-writing committees, House Ways and Means and Senate Finance, limits the number of potential veto points for tax expenditures on their way to being passed into law. This type of social spending is further advantaged by being part of the more complex revenue side of the budget process. In addition, because social tax expenditures are not subject to any aggregate or per taxpayer limit once they are passed, they function as an entitlement, since anyone can claim eligibility for these programs on their annual tax returns. Also, social tax expenditure programs, being administered by the IRS, are not connected to the federal bureaucracy. The IRS administers these programs "lightly," in that the agency creates program rules (which are not understood by the average voter) and in rare cases audits taxpayers who abuse or fabricate claims relating to tax expenditures. In total, social tax expenditures are considered "hidden" from the public view by their design, unusual policy process, and lack of overt bureaucratic administration.

The Puzzle of Public Opinion Toward the Hidden Welfare State

How do citizens form attitudes about social tax expenditures? Are these programs popular? If so, with whom? And why? In *The Submerged State* (2011), Suzanne Mettler examines how the rise of social tax subsidies for private welfare are understood (or not) by the mass public. Mettler argues that the unique characteristics of social tax expenditure programs—being passed off-budget as a tax subsidy and targeted at private social providers—interferes with citizens' ability to comprehend and respond to these types of benefits as government social welfare.[12] If citizens cannot learn about social tax expenditures from media reports on the national budget or interact with a federal agency in receiving benefits, she argues, then they are less likely to construct an informed opinion about these programs. This argument is backed up by an analysis from a 2008 survey that asked respondents whether they had "ever used a government social program."[13] Later in the survey, these same respondents were asked whether or not they had benefited from twenty-one different social policies—some from the public side, such as Social Security and food stamps, and others from the private side—for example, the Home Mortgage Interest Deduction (HMID) and tax deductions for 401(k)s.

The results indicated that respondents who used direct social programs were much more likely to report having used a government social program than respondents who had used a social tax expenditure program. Mettler concludes that beneficiaries of social tax expenditure programs do not recognize that they are receiving government benefits because of the "design and style of their delivery."[14] She goes on to argue that the design of social tax expenditures "obscure[s] the role of the government and exaggerate[s] that of the market, leaving citizens unaware of how power operates, unable to form meaningful opinions." A logical implication from this study is that citizens who benefit from federal tax expenditures should not be more supportive of these programs than citizens who do not benefit from them. After all, if social tax expenditure beneficiaries do not recognize the role of the government in providing these benefits, then they would be unable to connect their economic self-interest to supporting this type of government social spending on a survey. Therefore, homeowners who are making mortgage payments should not be more favorable toward the Home Mortgage Interest Deduction than renters, nor should workers who receive health care insurance through their employer be able to recognize and support the tax exclusion for employer-based health care payments more than citizens who buy insurance on the individual market or who receive government health care.

This line of argument presents an interesting puzzle in the study of American politics. Why would policymakers, who are motivated by reelection, create and expand social tax expenditure programs for which the beneficiaries are unable to assign them credit? A long line of studies show how much effort ambitious and reelection-minded legislators put into distributing federal benefits to voters and then claiming credit at election time.[15] Scholars find that social welfare programs are especially important for individual legislators and political parties in claiming credit for federal benefits.[16] As an example, the Democratic Party has long presented itself to the electorate as the creator and protector of the American welfare state. The electorate views the Democrats as "owning" issues such as health care, education, and assistance to the poor, and in turn Democratic candidates work to make elections about the economic security provided by social welfare programs.[17] One of the main rationales for the Republican Party's opposition to the expansion of public welfare is the widely held belief that these programs benefit Democratic constituencies and those voters return the favor in the voting booth.[18] In short, policymakers use social benefits and services to distribute benefits to loyal constituencies in order to improve their chances at reelection.

So then why would legislators spend the time and effort to create social programs that are "invisible" to the very groups that might reward them at the ballot box? What electoral benefit does a political party gain in passing a social tax expenditure program if voters assign credit for its material rewards to either their employer or the market? The political logic of invisible or hidden benefits is even more puzzling in light of how policymakers talk and act about social tax expenditure programs. President Donald Trump, during the lead-up to passing the tax reform bill, tweeted out to his followers that "there will be NO change to your 401(k). This has always been a great and popular middle-class tax break that works, and it stays!" The popularity of social tax expenditures is most on display when periodic efforts are made to trim the federal deficit through tax reform. Republican leaders, including Trump and House Speaker Paul Ryan, boosted the Tax Cuts and Jobs Act (TCJA) of 2017 as a piece of legislation that would "throw out" tax subsidies for special interests and "simplify the tax code" (code itself for cutting tax expenditures). Yet when all was said and done, the final bill actually increased the total number of federal tax expenditure programs. The death of federal tax expenditures, like Mark Twain's passing, was greatly exaggerated.

Former treasury secretary Robert Rubin, who served under President Bill Clinton, highlights the popularity of social tax expenditures with the following story: "Not long ago, a former senior official involved in the federal budget process told me that various senators used to meet with him periodically and argue for reducing tax expenditures. He would say that was a good idea, and then go down the list of large tax expenditures. At each one, the senator would say, 'Oh no, we can't do that,' and at some point the senator would repeat his proposition and the conversation would end."[19]

These programs are so popular that they have even been compared to Social Security, the most visible and beloved public social program. Charles Rangel, former chairman of the House Ways and Means Committee, discussed social tax expenditures during his 2007 budget negotiations with the George W. Bush administration. Rangel discussed these types of programs using the same terminology often invoked to discuss Social Security—as the "third rail" of American politics. A third-rail program is one so popular with the electorate that if you touch it you die (in other words, lose the next election). Rangel later recalled that some of the proposals of the President's Advisory Panel on Federal Tax Reform "were truly third rail. I mean you're not going to touch the churches and synagogues and the not-for-profits [that is, charitable contribution]. You're not going to touch local and state [deductions], and you're darn sure not going to touch the mortgage interest. And so the [administration] didn't do anything."[20] These anecdotes reveal that policymakers view public support for social tax expenditures as a major obstacle to reforming the national budget.

So while common sense around the Capitol Beltway may be that of course social tax expenditures are popular with voters, we are still left with no explanation for how, why, and with whom. How do political beliefs predict support for social tax subsidies? Does public opinion about these programs resemble attitudes toward traditional social spending, or is it more similar to attitudes toward tax policy? And how does the policy design of social tax expenditures structure public opinion toward these important federal social welfare programs?

Explaining Attitudes Toward Social Tax Expenditures: A Theoretical Argument

The important design feature of social tax expenditures is not their submersion within the formal policy process. Most citizens have very little knowledge of the legislative process on any important policy matter.[21] And so, while social tax expenditures are "off budget" and funneled through private organizations, these factors, not being widely understood, are inconsequential to how citizens form preferences toward social tax expenditures. If citizens do not know how a program is passed, who administers it, the annual costs, or its redistributive effects, then how do they formulate opinions on social tax expenditures? We argue that, when asked to provide an opinion on a social tax expenditure program, a respondent uses information from a basic description of the program to develop policy preferences.[22] A basic description of a social tax expenditure, such as a tax exclusion for health care insurance, provides three informational cues to voters: the delivery mechanism (the tax break), the policy area (health care), and the recipient (the worker with health benefits). These three components may cue politically relevant evaluations of the program that a citizen then uses to form preferences for the social tax expenditure.

The popularity of social tax expenditures has three sources: a policy design's appeal to citizens who favor limited government, its interference with attempts to politicize and racialize beneficiaries, and its signals to citizens about the deservingness of program beneficiaries. First, a social tax expenditure uses a conservative delivery mechanism (a tax break), thus generating support for federal social spending among citizens with antigovernment attitudes. Second, and relatedly, a social tax expenditure combines a tax subsidy with the funding of a traditionally liberal issue area (for example, income and housing security), thereby making it more difficult to politicize this category of spending, or at least more difficult to politicize along the lines of the standard left-right divide over the size and scope of government. Relatedly, these programs have not been politicized by political elites and the media. As a result, partisans and ideologues cannot easily use standard heuristics to evaluate these types of government social programs, and so they depend on "top of the head" considerations or self-interest instead to construct policy preferences. Third, the design of a social tax expenditure signals that program recipients are both taxpayers and workers—critical components of an aid recipient's perceived deservingness.

We do not argue that citizens begin with a blank slate every time they are asked about these programs, but rather that their attitudes toward this category of social spending are rather thin and therefore more reliant on using any and all information from the policy description provided in survey questions to help them form preferences toward them. In the following sections, we expound on these theoretical arguments for understanding the formation of public opinion toward social tax expenditure programs in the United States.

The American public is often thought of as "operationally liberal" but "philosophically conservative": Americans approve of spending to achieve specific social goals, but also tend to distrust government and to prefer that government be smaller and less intrusive.[23] As we discuss later in the book, the design of social tax expenditures reduces the cross-pressure on the significant number of citizens who hold some degree of antigovernment sentiment but also favor the financing of popular social goals. These citizens are ideologically conflicted when asked to evaluate direct social programs such as food stamps. They support assistance to the poor but are wary of granting the federal government more power.[24] Conservatives and Republicans are most likely to feel this cross-pressure, but it is also evident with many liberals.[25] A social tax expenditure pairs a conservative policy tool (a tax break) with a popular and liberal social policy, thereby reducing the ideological cross-pressure on these types of citizens.

Second, the design of a social tax expenditure program makes it more difficult for social spending of this type to be politicized. In an era of political party polarization and negative partisanship, partisan voters take policy positions on social welfare issues that align with their partisan identity.[26] Partisan voters are concerned about getting their policy positions "right," by taking the same position on policies as their party's elite. Social tax expenditure programs can remain relatively unpoliticized because of both the design of the programs and, relatedly, the lack of elite partisan cues about such expenditures. Social tax expenditures are relatively absent from the partisan political discourse not because these programs are passed through an off-budget process but rather because their design sends ideologically mixed cues to inattentive voters. And since many citizens cannot use their partisanship when forming attitudes toward these programs, we argue, they in turn default to more basic principles like self-interest to construct preferences for social tax subsidies.[27]

The design of social tax expenditures also increases support for this type of social spending by influencing how citizens perceive the deservingness of social welfare beneficiaries. One of the most significant factors in the formation of attitudes toward social welfare spending is perceptions of group deservingness.[28] A citizen who views a program's beneficiaries as deserving of government spending is likely to support the program. Groups that receive benefits through the tax code are viewed as having contributed to society in two ways—once as a worker in the economy and second as a tax-payer who contributes to the federal coffers. In fact, a citizen's awareness that recipients paid federal taxes meets one of Wim van Oorschot's criteria for deservingness—believing that these recipients will continue to contribute to the economy and the government.[29] Citizen evaluations of beneficiaries are particularly important for social tax expenditure programs aimed at the poor. Studies have shown that U.S. welfare programs struggle to gain widespread public support because the poor are highly racialized.[30] We expect that citizens will find beneficiaries of social tax expenditure programs more deserving of their government benefits than recipients of identical direct social spending programs and that these attitudes influence preferences for spending through the tax code.

The Implications of Studying Attitudes Toward Social Tax Expenditures for the Study of Public Opinion

Our study on public opinion toward social tax expenditures has implications for the study of public opinion toward government spending and social policy, our understanding of how a policy's design and delivery mechanism influence attitude formation, and the politics of the divided American welfare state. We theorize and demonstrate the importance of a program's delivery mechanism to the formation of attitudes toward social welfare spending. Our analysis throughout the book shows that a social welfare program's delivery mechanism changes how political beliefs are applied to policy preferences, reduces the cross-pressure on certain groups in favoring social spending, and frames program recipients as deserving of government assistance. Partisan beliefs, which for decades have been the most important factor in shaping preferences for direct social welfare programs, are relatively limited in their ability to structure and explain support for social tax expenditures. It is hard to imagine an area of modern American politics that is not shaped by partisanship, but the category of social spending through the tax code is one of those rare areas where partisanship, values, and ideology are of limited use in predicting support for a program.

The results reported in this book also have implications for understanding the political feasibility of antipoverty policies: they show that, at least to some extent, tax expenditure programs can be used to deliver monetary benefits to lower-income citizens while priming fewer of the racial stereotypes that often accompany such programs. The limitation of many social tax expenditures designed to help the poor is that they can only be used by poor citizens who are working and thus filing tax returns. But provided that tax credits are refundable, there is no a priori reason that tax expenditures must be regressive: we can certainly conceive of any number of downwardly distributing social benefits—to finance child care, pre-K education, or job training, for example—that could be delivered through the tax code. And as the United States becomes more racially and ethnically diverse, the already significant white backlash to federal social spending could intensify. Our results here show that social tax expenditures for the working poor might provide a politically sustainable mechanism to fund an increasingly diverse workforce in ways that direct public spending cannot.

In addition, we find that economic self-interest plays a large role in predicting support for a wide range of social tax expenditure programs. Contrary to existing studies, we argue that citizens have the capacity to support federal social tax expenditures because they are mindful of their own economic interests. As an example, citizens with active mortgages are more supportive of the Home Mortgage Interest Deduction than households that have paid off their homes or renting households. The salience of self-interest in structuring preferences for this type of social spending indicates that citizens are more likely to evaluate social tax expenditures through a tax policy lens than as an extension of traditional social welfare policy.[31] Our analysis indicates that the "hidden" welfare state is less hidden than theorized and that opposition to the private side of the divided welfare state is reduced, and support for it potentially increased, by the significant number of citizens who use these benefits.

Our analysis reveals that the private side of the divided social welfare state in America is as popular as the public side, if not more so. We conclude that one reason for the divided social welfare state is the widespread public support of social tax expenditures for private welfare. The popularity of public social welfare programs has been credited for slowing a conservative push for welfare retrenchment.[32] For example, the Bush administration's efforts at Social Security privatization failed owing to the popularity of Social Security with the American public. If this will always be the case, then the status quo—a divided social welfare state in which Americans support both universal public programs and tax subsidies for private social insurance—may be difficult to dislodge. The widespread popularity of social tax expenditures may maintain a divided social welfare state that both reduces and increases income inequality by funding progressive public programs as well as regressive tax expenditures. That popularity detracts from the federal government's ability to assuage rising inequality, not just by protecting existing regressive tax subsidies but also by reducing the public demand for more direct and progressive benefits.

Our findings here shed new light on the U.S. government's responsiveness to public opinion. We find not only that social tax expenditures are generally popular, but that these programs are supported by subpopulations that normally are not inclined to favor public social spending. There could very well be public demand for government solutions to address rising income inequality and economic insecurity, although it could take the form of citizens' preference for more social tax expenditures rather than expansions to the public welfare state targeted toward the elderly and poor. Studies show that Americans are more likely to favor public policies that support equal opportunity than policies targeted at equal outcomes. Social tax expenditures are palatable for citizens who want government to help people who help themselves. For decades antigovernment citizens have been cross-pressured by American social policy. These voters, many of whom are Republicans, conservatives, or citizens with low levels of trust in government, support spending on popular social goals such as affordable health insurance and quality education but are wary of big government and federal bureaucracies. The design of social tax expenditures takes some of the pressure off these citizens by providing financing for popular initiatives, but with only a light touch of government administration.

The Plan for the Book

In chapter 2, we explain the important role that social tax expenditure programs play in the divided American welfare state. We explain the conceptualization of a tax expenditure as a form of government spending and describe its role in financing the growth of the private welfare state. Next, we explore the growth of social tax expenditures both as a form of social insurance for most American families and as part of the federal budget for social welfare policy. The majority of households headed by working adults rely on federal social tax subsidies to help them pay for their health insurance, to save for retirement and college, and to reduce the cost of owning a home. We then explain how social tax expenditure programs—which have also become more prominent in the social welfare agendas of the political parties over time—diverge from public welfare programs in both design and function. These differences are important for understanding how citizens form attitudes about tax subsidies for social welfare that are different from their attitudes about traditional public social programs. The policy design features of a social tax expenditure program—not being administered by a federal bureaucracy and subsidizing private organizations, including businesses and religious institutions—appeal to highly cross-pressured subgroups such as Republicans, conservatives, individualists, and citizens who lack trust in the federal government.

In the subsequent chapters, we use a series of nationally representative surveys—conducted by YouGov America with the generous support of the Russell Sage Foundation and the Bucknell Institute for Public Policy—to examine many aspects of attitudes toward social policy in the United States.[33] These four surveys—conducted in August 2015, August 2016, July 2017, and October 2019—provide a novel series of data exploring attitudes toward social tax policies, attitudes toward the mechanisms through which government should deliver social benefits, and attitudes toward the beneficiaries of social assistance.

Chapter 3 begins to examine how Americans structure their attitudes toward social tax expenditures. In examining how beliefs about social tax expenditure categories are structured, we find that respondents view these programs similarly despite variations in policy area and mechanism (deduction versus credit). Next, we examine anti-tax sentiments, perceptions of program beneficiaries, partisanship, values, and economic self-interest as explanations for the popularity of social tax expenditures. We analyze these explanations in a full model of public attitudes toward social tax subsidies using YouGov's nationally representative surveys.

The results indicate that factors that traditionally predict support for direct public welfare programs do not have a consistent influence on preferences for social tax expenditures. However, variables that represent citizen self-interest in specific programs, such as the impact of homeownership on support for the HMID, is consistently significant and positively correlated with higher support for social tax expenditures. The analysis in this chapter supports our argument that social tax expenditure programs are popular, in part, because they do not polarize voters along partisan lines and beneficiaries are able to recognize their economic self-interest in these programs that contribute to their family's economic security.

Chapter 4 turns to a more direct comparison of direct and tax expenditure spending, seeking to understand differences in how the public evaluates social spending conducted through each method. Americans are of two minds when it comes to social spending: on the one hand, they generally approve of spending on many target groups and support solving the kinds of social problems that spending is typically designed to address. On the other hand, they tend to dislike the idea of "government intervention" and do not trust government to spend money effectively or efficiently. We argue that because of the means through which the benefits of social tax expenditures are delivered, these programs are more apt than direct spending programs to succeed in addressing this ambivalence toward social spending: they are generally focused on popular social goals, but they do so in a way that removes the specter of "big government." Through a series of survey experiments, we find that social programs financed through the tax code are more popular with citizens than otherwise identical programs financed through direct means. This is especially true for political conservatives and those who distrust the government, two groups of people typically reluctant to support a stronger direct federal role in solving social problems.

Chapter 5 turns to understanding how citizens perceive the beneficiaries of government assistance. Even above and beyond ideological or self-interest-type considerations, what people think of those who benefit from such programs may be the best predictor of their support for social spending programs. In short, people support spending on beneficiaries they perceive to be "deserving" and oppose spending on those they perceive as "undeserving." In the United States, deservingness is strongly tied to the idea of a work ethic: deserving beneficiaries are those who are working to help themselves; undeserving ones are those perceived as lazy or unwilling to work. The perception of whether a particular group is deserving or not is very often socially constructed, a function of citizens' different stereotypes and beliefs about people in that group. In addition, we argue, the perceived deservingness of beneficiaries of social assistance is also affected by the means through which they receive those benefits. We find through several survey experiments that beneficiaries of assistance delivered through the tax code are perceived on average as more deserving of the aid they receive than those who receive benefits directly. This difference stems, at least in part, from tax expenditures doing less to prime the racial stereotypes and prejudices that inform the discourse on deservingness in the United States.

In the concluding chapter, we outline some suggestions for extending our research on public attitudes toward social tax expenditure programs and for understanding the potential for social tax expenditures to reduce inequality and provide opportunity to a wider group of Americans. Other directions for further study include examining how citizens form opinions on other nontraditional types of federal spending, such as grants and loans, or how threats of automation in particular industries determine support for more public spending as opposed to tax subsidies tied to employment. A logical extension of our research is a study of how beneficiaries of social tax subsidies structure their preferences toward public social programs. Another area for future study is the way citizens who claim a strong white identity construct their attitudes toward spending through the tax code as opposed to spending on public welfare. This chapter also discusses the effect of the influential Tax Cuts and Jobs Act of 2017 on public attitudes toward major social tax expenditure programs. We explore the expansion of social tax expenditures into new areas, such as child care costs and assistance to renters, and the part played by such programs in expanding the federal government's role in addressing the social problems caused by rising inequality and growing economic dislocation. In the United States, the challenge of any such expansion of the government's role is doing so in a way that is palatable to a public that is generally skeptical and distrusting of government.

CHAPTER 2

The Politics of Private Social Welfare

WHAT ROLE DO social tax expenditures play in the divided American welfare state? How relevant is this type of federal social spending to the economic security of American families? And how does the policy design of social tax expenditure programs affect how citizens form attitudes about social spending?

We begin this chapter by explaining the concept of a federal tax expenditure and the role of these programs in subsidizing the private side of the divided welfare state. The increasing political importance of social tax expenditures is evidenced through their costs to the federal government and inclusion in both Republican and Democratic social welfare policy proposals. Next, we demonstrate the salience of social tax expenditures for American families' economic security. We illustrate that most families use federal tax subsidies to pay for health insurance and retirement pensions, save for college, and offset the costs of home mortgages. Finally, we describe the political differences between the policy designs of tax subsidies for private welfare and direct public social welfare programs. The unique characteristics of these programs contribute crucially to our understanding of how Americans construct their preferences toward social tax expenditures.

What Are Tax Expenditures?

A tax expenditure program, popularly known as a "tax break," is a government-sanctioned allocation of revenues targeted toward a specific group, such as low-income workers, or a special activity—owning a home or contributing to a 401(k), for example. The term "tax expenditure" is used by budget experts, tax economists, and policymakers to describe the hundreds of individual and corporate tax breaks in the federal tax code.[1] These financial experts use the term "expenditure" to classify a tax subsidy as something different from a cut in federal tax rates. Therefore, tax expenditures are not simple "loopholes" in the tax code, but rather "tax preferences"—specific and purposeful deviations from the tax code designed to subsidize particular activities or groups. A tax expenditure is similar to direct spending in that it must eventually be paid for through lower direct spending, higher taxes, or increased borrowing. We will hereafter refer to traditional or public social welfare programs such as Social Security, welfare, and Medicaid as "direct spending" programs and use the terms "social tax expenditure" or "social tax subsidy" to describe programs such as the deduction for 401(k) retirement plans.

Some popular examples of social tax expenditure programs are the HMID, deductions for property taxes, charitable contributions, and IRAs, the exclusions of contributions to employment-based health care and employment-sponsored retirement plans, and the EITC, to name just a few. These programs are all efforts by policymakers to use the tax code to finance and incentivize popular social goals, such as helping people pay for health care insurance, assisting with retirement security, subsidizing wages, and financing higher education. And just like direct spending programs, tax expenditure programs pick winners and losers and reward or punish certain behaviors. For example, home-buyers receive a whole set of generous tax subsidies, while renters do not. Workers who are offered employment-based benefits receive the accompanying federal subsidies, while workers who are not offered these fringe benefits do not receive federal assistance for their social insurance.

Although similar in some ways to traditional public social programs, tax expenditures differ in how they are designed, delivered, and administered by the federal government. Federal tax expenditures have been estimated and reported by the federal government since the late 1960s; a full list of tax expenditures is released annually by the Congressional Joint Committee on Taxation (JCT) and the Treasury Department. The JCT list is included as an appendix to the formal budget. The stated purpose of producing annual tax expenditure lists is to contrast and compare these programs with traditional programs in the formal budget.[2] A tax expenditure program for social welfare that forgoes $450 billion in collected tax revenues has a similar effect on the federal budget as a direct social spending program that is counted as a $450 billion budget outlay. Regardless, the federal government spends $450 billion to provide economic security, regardless of whether the money is forgone tax revenue or a direct expenditure.

Tax expenditures are created through a different policy process than that for regular social spending. Most tax expenditure programs originate in tax bills or omnibus bills in the revenue committees (which are not limited by substantive jurisdictions). The Senate Finance and House Ways and Means Committees serve as both the approving and appropriating committees for these programs, so they face fewer veto points than budgetary spending, which must pass through both substantive and budget committees. Not only does the narrow policy process allow for easier passage of tax expenditure programs than for direct spending programs, but once passed, this form of spending enjoys security from being cut. Since tax expenditures are a type of off-budget spending, they are not reevaluated every year during the budget process; tax expenditures can only be reduced or cut through a full legislative process that repeals or fundamentally alters the existing legislation. These programs also act as a form of entitlement spending, since any taxpayer can claim these benefits, and there is no limit to how many social tax expenditures can be claimed by a household or individual. The only bureaucratic agency a citizen interacts with in claiming these benefits is the IRS, through the process of filing annual tax returns. And reductions in both funding and personnel over the last decade have decreased the odds that a household will be audited by the IRS.[3] So, while the policy process favors social tax expenditures over direct social spending, we do not expect that citizens know or use this technical information in forming their attitudes toward spending through the tax code.

The Importance of Tax Expenditures to the Divided American Welfare State

In both their size and their impact on how citizens and employers behave, social tax expenditures are an important part of the policy landscape in the United States. One common way to measure the importance of social tax expenditures is through their budgetary impact. The United States is a tale of two welfare states—a public side that serves primarily the elderly and poor, and a private side that subsidizes primarily workers with employment-based benefits, homeowners, and citizens who save for health care expenses, higher education costs, and life insurance. As an example, the federal government provides health care insurance to the poor directly through Medicaid at a cost, in 2018, of $389 billion. In that same year, the federal government's subsidizing of employment-based health care insurance cost $146 billion.[4] Although these programs used different mechanisms or policy tools to deliver health care, in both cases federal revenue came off the books for the purpose of making health care insurance more available and affordable to citizens, and thus it is important to include both sides of the welfare state in measuring the size and scope of American social policy.

In comparative perspective, the size of the American welfare state depends on whether we examine the public side or the private side. Figure 2.1 shows how the United States compares with other advanced democracies in both public and private social spending as a percentage of gross domestic product (GDP).[5] U.S. annual spending on public social welfare programs was 18.7 percent of GDP in 2018. American spending on public welfare is below the international average (20.9 percent of GDP) and higher than only two other countries in the figure—Switzerland and Canada. Generous welfare states such as Denmark and France spent over ten percentage points more of their GDP on social welfare than did the United States. These data align with historical trends: the United States has long been a "laggard" or "small" welfare state in comparisons across countries.[6] Whether measured through spending or number of beneficiaries, public social welfare programs in the United States are limited compared to most other advanced democracies in the world.

In contrast, the United States ranks first among these nations in private-sector social welfare expenditures. In 2018, the United States spent

Figure 2.1 An International Comparison of National Social Spending as a Percentage of GDP, 2018

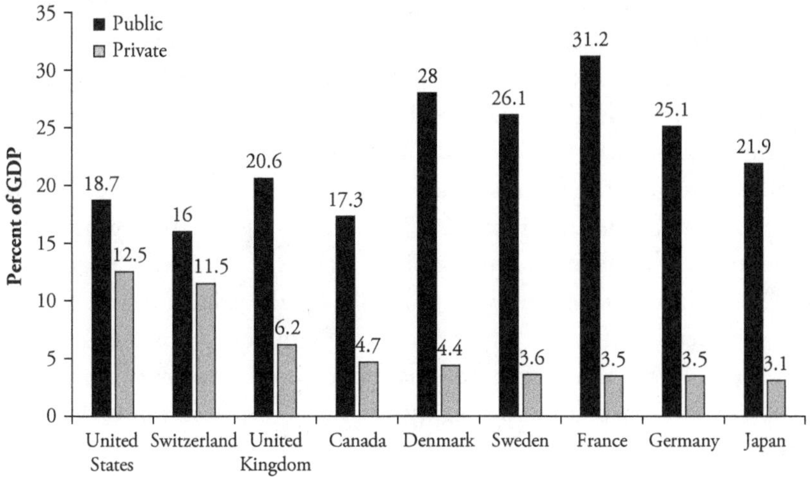

Source: Organization for Economic Cooperation and Development 2020.

12.5 percent of national GDP on private social welfare, which was four times the international average (3 percent of GDP). The United States spends twice as much on the private provision of social insurance compared to the United Kingdom and almost three times as much as Canada. An Organization for Economic Cooperation and Development (OECD) report from 2010 showed that the United States spent the most on social tax expenditures of any country in the industrialized world.[7]

It is no coincidence that the United States is an international leader in private social spending: it does so by design, mainly through the large and increasing number of social subsidies in the tax code. For example, the United States has the largest private health care system in the world; correspondingly, it allocated over $200 billion to various health care insurance tax subsidies in 2018 alone. Also, hundreds of millions of U.S. citizens contribute to private pensions every year, and these contributions are subsidized through a number of tax expenditures whose cost exceeds $300 billion per year. Another item to notice in figure 2.1 is the relative balance between spending on public and private social welfare in the United States compared to other advanced nations. The United States allocates a relatively equal percentage of the economy to public versus private social welfare programs—there is only a six-percentage-point gap. In most European countries, spending on public welfare programs dwarfs expenditures on private benefits—the OECD average is a public spending gap of 17.6 percent. So both as a singular category and in relation to public social spending, the U.S. private social state is sizable.

This type of social spending also represents a significant portion of the national budget. The federal government spent over $1 trillion on all tax expenditures in the 2019 fiscal year, and these programs have grown as a proportion of all federal spending since 1970. The rise in the tax expenditure budget has been driven primarily by the addition and expansion of social welfare tax expenditures for families. Christopher Faricy has shown that the number of social tax expenditures rose from thirty programs in 1970 to just under eighty by 2012.[8] Over the last three decades, the federal government has added new programs to help families save and pay for their children's college education (for example, the HOPE Scholarship Tax Credit) and health care expenses in the form of Health Savings Accounts (HSAs), as well as new programs to help the uninsured purchase health care insurance. Existing programs, such as the EITC, credits for contributions to 401(k)s and IRAs, and the exclusion for employment-based health care insurance, have also been expanded.

The growth of federal tax subsidies has fueled the rise of the private social welfare state in the United States. Figure 2.2 shows the increase of overall U.S. tax expenditures as a percentage of the overall federal budget from 1979 to 2017 by tracking annual tax expenditures over tax expenditures plus annual budget authority. These data are from the Policy Agendas Project data on the national budget. In the late 1970s, tax expenditures represented $1 out of every $5 spent by the federal government. That rose quickly to just under 30 percent by 1986. The 1986 Tax Reform Act cut a large number of business-related tax expenditures and left the expenditures for social welfare untouched in exchange for reduced individual and corporate tax rates, resulting in an overall drop in the tax expenditure budget. The value of federal tax expenditures increased throughout the remaining decades and as of 2017 represented over 30 percent of total federal spending (tax expenditures plus regular budgetary spending). It is important to note the resiliency of social tax expenditures compared to business tax breaks: if all tax expenditures are divided into two categories—ones for social welfare

Figure 2.2 U.S. Tax Expenditures as a Percentage of the Total Federal Budget, 1979–2017

Source: Policy Agendas Project data, available at https://www.comparativeagendas.net/tool?project=us (accessed September 24, 2020).

and ones for nonsocial welfare—social tax expenditures as a percentage of all tax expenditures doubled from 40 to 80 percent between 1974 and 2012.[9]

Some of the more popular tax expenditure programs, such as the exclusion for employment-based health care insurance and the capital gains deduction, cost hundreds of billions of dollars every year in forgone revenue to the federal government. The ten most expensive tax expenditure programs for the fiscal year 2018 are listed in table 2.1. The majority of these programs are social benefits for households, not tax breaks for businesses or corporations. This is also true of the larger universe of programs.[10] The three largest social tax expenditure programs are connected to employment based social insurance (health care and pensions) and cost the federal government over $376 billion in 2018. The government also spent over $131 billion on just the home mortgage interest and property tax deductions. As we will see, the seven most expensive social tax expenditures are regressive federal programs that provide the most assistance to the wealthiest citizens. (The regressive design of many social tax expenditures

Table 2.1 The Ten Most Expensive Federal Tax Expenditure Programs, 2018

Program	Cost (in Billions of Dollars)
Exclusion of employment-based contributions for health care	235.8
Exclusion of imputed rental income	112.7
Deferral of income from controlled foreign corporations	112.6
Capital gains	108.6
Defined-benefit employer pensions	71.0
Defined-contribution employer pensions	69.4
Mortgage interest	68.1
Earned Income Tax Credit	63.6
Deductible state and local taxes	63.3
Child tax credit	54.3

Source: Joint Committee on Taxation 2019.

is also reflected in the larger universe of tax expenditure programs.) However, two of the most expensive antipoverty programs can also be found in the federal tax code—the EITC and the Child Care Tax Credit.

The Expanded Role of Tax Expenditures in Democratic and Republican Social Welfare Policies

Another way to explain the rise of tax expenditures is through an examination of the political parties' social welfare platforms and policy positions over time. There were very few mentions of social tax expenditures in political party platforms and campaign speeches throughout the 1950s and 1960s. The politics of social welfare policy during this period was dominated by Democratic attempts to expand the New Deal programs and by Republicans' grudging acceptance of these popular programs. Economic recessions and inflationary pressures in the 1970s, however, changed the politics of social welfare policy.

The rise of the conservative movement within the Republican Party, starting with the 1964 presidential campaign of Senator Barry Goldwater, shifted the party's fiscal policy from balanced budgets to tax-cutting. Republicans recognized that until the pace of federal social spending was slowed, there would be a hard floor on how much federal taxes could be cut. Since simply proposing cuts to popular social programs was politically unpopular, a new strategy was necessary. The Republican Party started to propose new tax expenditure programs for health care and pensions rather than directly attacking popular programs such as Social Security.[11] This was part of the Republican "starve the beast" strategy of cutting taxes to reduce future federal revenue that could be used for social welfare programs that were championed by Democrats and popular with the electorate.[12] Social tax expenditures played a crucial role in this political strategy, since they both reduced federal revenues and provided a private alternative to public social welfare programs.

Reagan's 1980 presidential campaign offered a number of new and expanded social tax expenditures for old-age pensions, health care insurance, and higher education. The Reagan social welfare policy agenda turned away from Eisenhower's and Nixon's reluctant acceptance of direct social welfare programs and offered the American public a federally funded private alternative. The Reagan playbook on social welfare policy was continued by George H. W. Bush in the 1988 presidential campaign. The Republican Party had finally found a winning formula in the 1980s to counter the Democratic Party's electoral success of proposing popular social benefits to voters—proposing social tax expenditures instead.

The nation's political turn to the right resulted in the movement of the Democratic Party to the ideological middle and the ascendance of the "New Democrat," who found middle ground between liberal Democrats and conservative Republicans. President Bill Clinton, the most successful of the New Democrats, promised to "end welfare as we know it" and surrounded himself with economic advisers such as Larry Summers, who pushed tax expenditures onto the Democratic Party's social welfare agenda.[13] In fact, Summers once "touted the promotion of social values through the tax code as the highlight of the Clinton administration's tax policy."[14] President Clinton's early policy failures (for example, health care reform and the "don't ask don't tell" policy in the military) helped Republicans take control of the legislative branch in the midterm elections of 1998. President Clinton worked with the new Republican Congress to expand the EITC and added new tax expenditure programs to help families pay for the rising cost of higher education. These programs fit with Clinton's New Democrat agenda and helped him expand social spending during a period of divided government. By the end of Clinton's two terms in the White House, both political parties were promoting social tax expenditure programs as an example of good social policies that were also good politics.

George W. Bush expanded upon the Reagan legacy by running on a "compassionate conservative" agenda that sought to present Republican alternatives to historically Democratic issues such as education and social insurance. One example of this "compassionate conservative" policy is the new Health Savings Accounts passed as part of the Medicare Prescription Drug, Improvement, and Modernization Act of 2003. Part of a broader effort to move more of Medicare to the private sector, this new tax expenditure program for health care allowed citizens who were covered by high-deductible plans to put money in a savings account that would roll over and could be used for specified medical expenses.[15] The Bush administration and congressional Republicans were less successful in privatizing Social Security through the strategy of using a new consolidated tax expenditure program for private pensions. Republicans in Congress were hesitant about reforming such a wildly popular program right before the midterm election in 2006. However, Republicans did create new tax expenditure programs for disaster relief after both 9/11 and Hurricane Katrina.[16] In short, the Bush administration did not encounter a problem that it did not answer with the introduction of new or expanded tax expenditure programs.

The Obama administration's approach to social welfare policy is best represented by the signature health care reform package popularly known as Obamacare, which blended expansions to direct public programs and new tax expenditures for private welfare. The Patient Protection and Affordable Care Act signed in 2010 extended health care insurance to the uninsured through two main mechanisms: an expansion of Medicaid and a set of new health care tax expenditures aimed at reducing the cost for both employers and employees to purchase health care on the new insurance markets. In addition, individuals whose income was at or just above the poverty line were eligible for new tax subsidies that helped with health insurance premium costs. This mixed approach to spending was also evident in the Obama administration's American Recovery and Reinvestment Act of 2009, which provided direct federal assistance as well as a host of new tax expenditures for reducing college costs, assisting first-time home-buyers, subsidizing unemployment insurance, and promoting renewable energy. President Obama continued the Clinton social policy trend of expanding both sides of the divided welfare state with a mixture of tax expenditures and enlarged public programs. In conclusion, the divided American welfare state has become increasingly tilted toward the private side through new and expanded tax expenditure offerings over the last forty years.

The Importance of Social Tax Expenditures to American Families' Economic Security

There are four main ways in which federal tax expenditures assist families in obtaining economic security: social insurance, capital investments, savings programs, and wage subsidies. The first form of federal assistance operates through tax exclusions and deductions associated with employment-based social insurance. According to estimates from the Employee Benefit Research Institute (EBRI), 160 million Americans used employment-based health insurance in 2016, and 140 million were enrolled in company-sponsored retirement plans.[17] In comparison, 65.1 million people received benefits from the Social Security Administration in the same year.[18] The Bureau of Labor Statistics reports that 86 percent of all workers had access to an employment-sponsored retirement plan in 2019 (defined-contribution or defined-benefit) and that 52 percent of workers were enrolled in a medical care plan. The workers enrolled in these programs were able to exclude their contributions (a form of income) from the income they reported for tax purposes. The federal tax exclusions and deductions for these types of employment-based benefits are some of the largest tax breaks in the tax code.

The second mechanism through which federal social tax expenditures contribute to family economic security is the subsidizing of wealth accumulation through assets. A simple definition of wealth is a household's income plus assets. The most important and often only asset owned by the typical American family is their home.[19] In 2018, around 80 million homeowners held an active mortgage, which translates into a home-ownership rate of just under 65 percent.[20] Two of the largest social tax expenditures are deductions for home mortgage interest and property taxes. Our own 2015 survey shows that, of those respondents who itemized, 60.6 percent reported making a home mortgage payment. Another tax expenditure related to homeownership, the property tax deduction, was claimed by 69 percent of our respondents who itemized their annual tax returns. These two programs are skewed to providing the most benefits to the richest households. According to the IRS, three out of four households making over $100,000 claim the HMID for an average per return of over $10,000.[21] In contrast, only 4 percent of households making under $20,000 claimed the HMID; among those who did, the average benefit was only $278.

The third method through which social tax expenditures assist many families with economic security is to help them invest in the stock market. The federal tax code encourages families to invest in the stock market through retirement plans such as IRAs and 401(k)s. Two types of IRAs qualify for tax subsidies—the traditional IRA and the Roth IRA. Employees contribute to 401(k) plans with pretax dollars, which are therefore deductible from their taxable income. In 2018, 54 million workers, or around 32 percent of the U.S. workforce, were enrolled in 401(k) accounts.[22] These programs assist mainly wealthier professionals, higher percentages of whom enroll in IRAs and 401(k)s and make large contributions, thus gaining higher tax subsidies.

The final major category of social tax expenditures is designed to incentivize families to save their income for major expenses such as large medical bills or their children's college tuition. There are two major tax expenditure programs for health care costs—the deduction for high medical expenses and the HSA deduction. The first is mainly used by older people, who spend more annually on medical care, and the second is used by middle-class and wealthier families who save for their annual medical expenses. Our survey shows that 40 percent of itemizers claimed the tax break for significant out-of-pocket health care costs in 2015.

A number of programs also help families pay for higher education costs, including the HOPE Scholarship Tax Credit and the Lifetime Learning Credit. In addition, there are tax breaks for parents with college-age students (eighteen to twenty-three years old), for people who pay student loan interest, and for those who contribute to 529 plans and Coverdell Education Savings Accounts (ESAs). According to the Department of Education, over 14 million citizens were enrolled in 529 plans in 2018. These programs cost the federal government over $35 billion in 2018.

The number of American households using social tax subsidies is especially considerable when compared to public programs. While around three in five households use the largest social tax expenditures, only one in five families benefit from direct public social spending. Recent data from 2018 indicate that around 25 percent of households benefit in some way from Social Security (or supplemental security income [SSI]), 15 percent are enrolled in Medicare, and 20 percent receive Medicaid benefits.[23] In contrast, over 22 million low-income workers received a wage subsidy in 2018 through the Earned Income Tax Credit, according to IRS estimates. Using a national survey, Suzanne Mettler and Jeffrey Stonecash show that the percentage of Americans who used public programs in 2005 was considerably lower: 9.1 percent claimed that they had recently received welfare payments, 6.3 percent had children enrolled in Head Start, 6.5 percent lived in public housing, 12.5 percent received food stamps, and 9.5 percent were enrolled in Medicaid.[24] In conclusion, social tax expenditures are some of the most widely used programs for social insurance, asset accumulation, savings, and wage subsidies in the federal policy landscape.

Tax Expenditures as a Conservative Policy Tool

A policy tool is an instrument used by the government to pursue a desired outcome.[25] Public policy scholars argue that the government can pursue a policy goal using a number of different mechanisms; to make college affordable, for instance, the government can make federal loans available, subsidize private loans, make direct payments, deliver direct services, or offer tax subsidies. How a government chooses to finance a policy goal matters for the politics of when, what, and who benefits from that policy. Direct cash assistance to needy citizens, for example, reflects a fundamentally "liberal" approach to government: in this view, a larger and more expansive government provides direct relief to its citizens. Though tax expenditures can be used to achieve both conservative and liberal social goals, a case can be made that the design and structure of the programs themselves reflect a fundamentally conservative approach to the proper size and scope of the federal government.

First, unlike many public programs that directly provide services or cash assistance, a social tax expenditure is a tax subsidy. Though not designed as an across-the-board rate cut, tax expenditures do reduce the total revenue collected by the federal government and allow citizens to pay less in federal taxes each year. Though these programs need not target traditionally conservative policy goals (and as noted, many Democratic leaders have used tax expenditures to serve their own aims), they almost universally comport with a conservative desire to lower the federal tax burden for Americans.

Second, and relatedly, these programs are government subsidies targeted toward the private sector of the economy. The major social tax expenditures finance employer provisions of social insurance and assist individuals with savings plans; through the charitable contribution deduction, they also support private or nonprofit organizations that provide insurance and social benefits. A social tax expenditure is often presented to citizens by policymakers as a private-sector market solution to economic insecurity problems. There has long been a partisan and ideological divide over whether the government or the private market should take the lead in the provision of social welfare goods and services.[26] Democrats show higher levels of relative trust in the federal government than Republicans, and Republicans, on average, report more trust in businesses, corporations, and the private sector than Democrats.[27] By privileging private-sector market solutions to social problems, tax expenditures also comport with a desire to expand the reach of the private sector vis-à-vis government in shaping behavior and how society conducts its business.

Finally, another conservative characteristic of a social tax expenditure program is that it does not require the administration of a federal bureaucracy. Since social tax expenditures are executed through the tax code, there is no formal government agency (outside of the light touch of the IRS) that delivers these federal benefits to constituencies. In the absence of any need for a federal bureaucratic agency to administer these programs, proponents can present this type of spending as a "small-government" solution to the problem of making social insurance affordable. Many of these programs encourage and incentivize savings accounts for major expenses such as health care (for example, HSAs) and higher education (ESAs). Social tax expenditures such as these are presented to citizens as rewarding personal responsibility and prudence— once again signaling conservative principles to people with small-government leanings. In short, a tax break that subsidizes private providers and individuals is a type of federal social spending that conservatives and citizens with antigovernment sentiments can learn to love (or at least to not hate).

The Different Beneficiaries of Direct Social Spending and Social Tax Subsidies

Perhaps the most important difference between direct social spending and social tax expenditures is that, for a number of reasons, most major tax expenditures in the United States distribute wealth upward. First, many major tax expenditures are available only to people working in benefits-eligible jobs for employers who voluntarily offer workplace benefits. White-collar and other professional workers are more likely to be offered employment benefits as part of their compensation. Second, larger benefits accrue to wealthier people in higher tax brackets, and the largest deductions for mortgage interest go to those with the most expensive homes, the largest retirement tax subsidies go to those who can save the most for retirement, and so on. Finally, some tax expenditures go to those who can afford to do things that others cannot, such as save for unexpected medical expenses or donate large amounts to charities of their choice.

Public social programs in the United States largely benefit one of two groups—the elderly or the poor. So how citizens feel about those two groups, and especially about their deservingness, informs their attitudes toward public social welfare programs.[28] A significant number of studies now show that the poor, and programs that serve the poor, are racialized.[29] We have theorized that the design of social tax expenditures cues citizens to consider social tax expenditure beneficiaries as workers and taxpayers and therefore as deserving of government benefits. These beneficiaries also are advantaged by their diversity and socioeconomic privilege in the political arena. The groups that benefit from social tax expenditure programs are more varied, and subpopulations not associated with traditional public welfare are favored by these programs. The large assortment of different groups that benefit from social tax expenditures makes it difficult to politicize the recipients as a category. In addition, the modal recipient of employment-based social insurance is a wealthy, white professional working in a large company—characteristics contrary to the stereotypes associated with public welfare recipients.

Table 2.2 A Comparison of Users of Public and Employment-Based Health Insurance in the United States, 2016

	Employment-Based Insurance	Public Insurance	Percentage-Point Difference
Race/ethnicity			
White	67.0%	17.0%	50.0%
Black	45.3	34.1	11.2
Latino	39.2	29.3	9.9
Other	58.2	20.8	37.4
Occupation			
Managerial and professional	43.7	22.7	21.0
Service	13.4	29.5	−16.1
Sales and office	23.7	25.8	−2.1
Farming, fishing, and forestry	0.4	1.2	−0.8
Construction, extraction, and maintenance	7.6	8.6	−1.0
Production, transportation, and material moving	11.2	12.2	−1.0
Earnings			
Less than $10,000	11.1	49.6	−38.5
$10,000 to $19,999	17.8	44.6	−26.8
$20,000 to $29,999	32.8	34.4	−1.6
$30,000 to $30,999	48.6	25.6	23.0
$40,000 to $49,999	59.1	20.8	38.3
$50,000 to $74,999	71.4	14.0	57.4
$75,000 or more	84.7	7.9	76.8

Source: Employee Benefit Research Institute 2016.

In the following sections, we examine in more detail the differences between beneficiaries of direct welfare and social tax expenditure programs and extrapolate how these differences influence the construction of public opinion toward social spending. We show in table 2.2 the differences between groups that use employment-based health insurance (and the corresponding federal tax exclusions) and the populations that rely on public health insurance such as Medicaid. There are clear socioeconomic differences in who benefits from tax expenditures for private health insurance and those who are enrolled in public plans. First, there are stark racial differences between users of public versus private health insurance. White citizens disproportionately use private-sector health insurance (67 percent) as compared to public insurance (17 percent)—a fifty-point gap. Black and Latino citizens are likely to use private and public health programs more evenly (with around a ten-point gap in usage) and are enrolled in employment-based programs in much smaller numbers than white workers (a 20 to 25 percent difference). These racial gaps are related to occupational differences between the two kinds of users.

Workers' socioeconomic status is the most important determinant of whether or not they have access to employment-based benefits and the corresponding federal tax subsidies. Professional workers are offered and enroll in employment-based health insurance at higher rates than blue-collar workers, many of whom use public health insurance, buy health insurance on the individual market, or are simply uninsured or underinsured. Out of the six occupational categories listed in table 2.2, *only* managers and professionals use private health insurance at a higher rate than public health insurance, and they do so at double the rate they use public plans. Every other occupational group on this list is more reliant on public health programs than private insurance. This socioeconomic trend is also reflected by household income level. In table 2.2, income correlates highly with enrollment in employment-based health care insurance. For example, only 11 percent of those at the lowest income level (under $10,000) use employment-based insurance, while half are enrolled in public health care plans. In comparison, at the highest income level (over $75,000), 85 percent use employment-based insurance compared to only 8 percent who rely on public health programs. These patterns also appear in other employment-based benefits, such as retirement plans, life insurance, and programs that help pay for further training and education. The implication here is that attitudes toward social tax expenditures are less likely to be driven by public feelings toward one or two groups, since there is a wide array of beneficiaries. In addition, social tax expenditures are less likely to be racialized given their importance to the safety net of white families and lower usage by black and Latino families.

These socioeconomic differences in access to federal social tax expenditures map onto the income distributional effects of the programs (see figure 2.3). In contrast to public social spending, the major tax expenditure programs distribute federal money up the income ladder to wealthier citizens. Tax subsidies have a wide range of beneficiaries, but they disproportionately assist homeowners, the wealthy, and corporations. Figure 2.3 uses Treasury Department data to show the distributional impact

Figure 2.3 Income Distribution of Major Individual Tax Expenditures, 2013

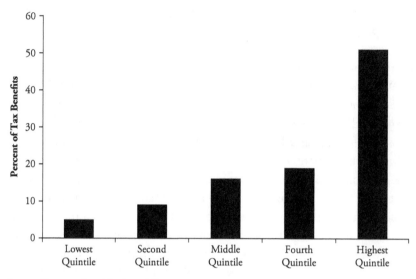

Source: Congressional Budget Office 2013.

of subsidies delivered through the tax code. The horizontal axis shows the population grouped into income quintiles. The richest families, those in the top 20 percent, receive over half of the total benefits. The middle class receives only 16 percent of overall tax benefits, and only 5 percent accrues to the poorest households.

This distributional impact is driven not just by eligibility for and use of social tax expenditure programs. The overall federal income tax structure is progressive: marginal tax rates increase as a taxpayer's income increases. Since exclusions, exemptions, and deductions are levied against a progressive tax rate structure, the value of these tax provisions increases as a taxpayer's income goes up. The current federal individual income tax rate structure ranges from 10 to 37 percent, and therefore the value of a $1,000 deduction can range from $100 for taxpayers in the lowest bracket to $370 for taxpayers in the highest bracket. And since higher-income individuals often deduct or exclude more money from their income taxes, the aggregate value of these programs is even higher. In addition, fewer than half of all taxpayers make enough annual income to itemize their tax returns. Wealthier taxpayers are more likely to itemize their taxes and therefore have more opportunity to claim more tax expenditure benefits.

Conclusion

Hundreds of millions of Americans annually rely on federal tax subsidies so that they and their families can afford health care insurance, large medical expenses, contributions to retirement plans, college, student loan payments, housing and property costs, and child care costs; they rely as well on the wage assistance provided by these subsidies. The average working family relies on tax subsidies as the main form of government assistance for their social insurance and savings, both of which are central to economic security.

Tax expenditures that finance private social welfare have grown as a proportion of social spending and the national budget. Additionally, policymakers have increasingly incorporated new social tax expenditure programs into their proposed plans for social welfare policy, such as Republicans' "compassionate conservatism" agenda and Democratic attempts to gain moderate and conservative support for their health care and education proposals. In short, social tax expenditure programs have become more important in both the lives of American households and the federal government's effort to provide citizens with economic security. However, scholarship on public opinion about social welfare policy has not kept up with these changes in the divided welfare state.

In this chapter, we discussed the substantial differences in how social tax subsidies and direct public welfare programs are designed. We have argued that these design differences are important to understanding how the public formation of attitudes toward tax subsidies varies from traditional accounts of public preferences toward social spending. Social tax expenditure programs differ from direct public welfare programs in that they take the form of off-budget spending, they finance private organizations, and they have regressive income distribution effects. In addition, tax expenditures tend to benefit recipients who are white, more likely to be working in full-time, benefits-eligible positions, and more likely to be in professional white-collar occupations.

Because of these differences, how Americans construct attitudes toward social tax expenditures are very different from how they form preferences with respect to public welfare. We expect that social tax subsidies will be popular because they provide indirect government assistance for popular social goals: providing social benefits while avoiding the specter of "big government" involvement in the private sector. In the next chapter, we test how traditional attitudinal factors such as partisanship, values, and self-interest structure preferences for social tax expenditure programs. The factors that predict support for direct social spending programs, we find, behave differently when applied to social tax expenditures.

CHAPTER 3

Attitudes Toward Social Tax Expenditures

SO FAR, WE have seen that while tax expenditure programs may serve similar populations and work to achieve similar goals as direct spending programs, they often have different economic and social impacts: many of the largest tax expenditures are distributed upward, reinforce inequality, and transfer power over the distribution of benefits to the private sector. We have also argued that because of the unique nature of their delivery, the public may view social tax expenditures differently than they view comparable direct social welfare programs and direct spending more generally.

In this chapter, we begin our examination of public opinion about tax expenditure programs by relying on a series of nationally representative surveys to explore public support and correlates of that support for seven major tax expenditure programs. We find that tax expenditure programs are generally quite popular with the American public. This popularity extends to programs that are both upwardly and downwardly distributing, serve a variety of different ends, and are delivered through both tax deductions and tax credits.

Many of the predictors of support for tax expenditure programs are similar to those for direct spending programs, but we also see important differences. Taken together, these differences begin to explain the high levels of support for social benefits delivered through the tax code. In particular, we see that the base of support for tax expenditure programs appears to be broader than that for direct spending programs, that partisan differences in support are often muted, and that factors such as political values often play a limited role in determining who supports these programs and who does not. Citizens whose antigovernment sentiment leads them to be less supportive of direct social spending are usually supportive of social tax expenditures.

Public Opinion and Social Tax Expenditures

To examine public support for social tax expenditures, we first rely on data from a nationally representative survey conducted by YouGov for the Bucknell Institute for Public Policy in October 2019. This survey asked respondents how much they supported seven major tax expenditures that, taken together, account for a large majority of all federal dollars spent through the tax code. These seven tax subsidies finance support for employment-based health care, 401(k)s, charitable contributions, home mortgage interest payments, college savings, and student loan debt and provide a low wage subsidy (analogous to the Earned Income Tax Credit).

Respondents were asked: "Here is a list of some programs that can allow people to reduce their federal income tax. Please tell me whether you strongly support, support, neither support nor oppose, or strongly oppose, each program":[1]

1 A tax break that allows citizens to pay no federal income tax on their contributions to their employer-sponsored health care plan
2 A tax break that allows citizens to reduce the amount they pay in income taxes based on how much they pay in interest on their home mortgage
3 A tax break that subsidizes the wages of low-income earners by increasing the size of their federal income tax refund
4 A tax break that allows citizens to pay no federal income tax on the amount they contribute to an employer-sponsored retirement plan
5 A tax break that allows parents to reduce the amount they pay in income taxes based on how much they pay for their children's college education
6 A tax break that allows citizens to reduce the amount they pay in income taxes based on how much they pay in interest on their student loans
7 A tax break that allows citizens to reduce the amount they pay in income taxes for the money they spend on child care for their children

Figure 3.1 Public Opinion Toward Social Tax Expenditures, 2019

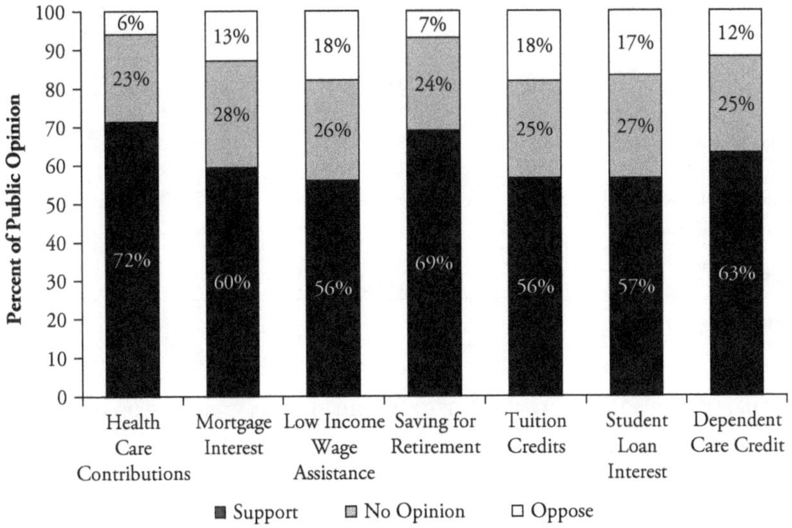

Source: YouGov survey, October 2019.

These programs differ in their design and effects. As discussed in chapter 2, three of these subsidies—the exclusion for contributing to a private health insurance plan, the deduction for paying mortgage interest, and the subsidies for saving for retirement through an employer-sponsored plan—are heavily upwardly distributing. The low-wage subsidy program distributes nearly all of its benefits to those near the bottom of the income distribution. Figure 3.1 presents levels of support for these programs. The first thing to note is that all of these programs received majority support— indeed, the most remarkable feature of public opinion toward social tax subsidies is how unremarkable the level of support for these programs is. Support varies a bit by program—from around 70 percent for the health care and retirement credits to around 60 percent for the other programs. But support is high for all of them: none of the tax expenditure programs met with more than 18 percent opposition among respondents. A high percentage of respondents (on average around one in five Americans) neither support nor oppose the average social welfare tax subsidy. The public's uncertainty about social tax expenditures is much higher than its uncertainty about public social welfare programs. Though apples-to-apples comparisons are difficult, levels of support for these programs rival support for

Table 3.1 Principal-Factor Analysis of Tax Expenditure Programs, 2019

	Factor 1 (Loading)	Factor 2 (Loading)
Health care contributions	0.19	0.54
Mortgage interest	0.43	0.36
Low-wage income assistance	0.46	0.13
Saving for retirement	0.27	0.57
Tuition credits	0.57	0.20
Student loan interest	0.71	0.20
Dependent care credit	0.63	0.21
Eigenvalue	1.86	0.90

Source: YouGov survey, October 2019.

popular downwardly distributing programs such as spending on education, public health, and Social Security.

How Tax Expenditure Beliefs Are Structured

How do citizens organize their beliefs on tax expenditures? Do they view these programs discretely, in response to specific policy areas, in terms of how benefits are delivered (through a deduction or credit), according to their likely beneficiaries, or as part of a general class of "tax breaks"?

As a first-pass answer to this question, table 3.1 presents the results of a principal-components factor analysis (with varimax rotation) of the seven tax expenditure programs. This analysis returns only one factor with an Eigenvalue greater than 1, with all seven tax breaks loading on this main factor. This finding suggests that respondents expressed support or opposition to tax breaks broadly defined rather than making fine-grained distinctions between them. There is some evidence that the tax breaks designed to help families and students most directly (student loan interest, tuition credits, and dependent day care) load most strongly together. This suggests that respondents may have made some distinction between different types of tax breaks based on who they are designed to help, though the other two tax breaks that load most strongly on this factor, the mortgage interest deduction and the credit providing low-wage income assistance, share little in common with these three factors in terms of beneficiaries or distributive outcomes.

But in general, the relative similarity in levels of support across tax break programs, combined with the results of this factor analysis, suggests that respondents were not necessarily making fine-grained distinctions between beneficiaries in deciding what tax breaks to support or oppose. It also shows fairly clearly that people made no fine-grained distinctions between the measures used to deliver tax expenditures—a credit or a deduction, for example. This stands somewhat in contrast to research on direct spending, which shows that cross-sectionally—if not necessarily over time—public opinion on direct spending programs is multidimensional.[2]

Why Are Tax Expenditure Programs Popular?

We see fairly high levels of support for tax expenditure programs regardless of the area they finance or their beneficiaries. In the public spending sphere, by contrast, research typically shows fairly high levels of support for the working poor and other populations seen as sympathetic or deserving, but tepid support for programs seen as benefiting the wealthy or other "underserving" interests.[3] One reason for the popularity of tax expenditure programs in our survey has to do, of course, with the nature of the questions themselves. Just as support for direct public programs goes down when people are reminded that someone must pay for any additional spending, our questions did not remind respondents that tax expenditure programs have costs. Another reason for the popularity of the tax expenditure programs is that some of them, much like some of the direct spending programs, target beneficiaries who are perceived as deserving of support—parents and children, for instance. In the following sections, we examine various explanations for the popularity of social tax expenditures, including anti-tax sentiments, policy ignorance, and traditional factors such as partisanship, values, and self-interest.

Is the United States a "Taxophobic" Nation?

Tax expenditures of all kinds may be popular because they are seen as reducing taxes, and the United States is often regarded as a "taxophobic" country, ready to do anything to reduce our collective tax bill.[4] But a good bit of research suggests that the American public, while clearly not as supportive of higher taxes as the populations of many Western European countries, is a more tax-tolerant nation than is often claimed. Vanessa Williamson's excellent analysis, for example, shows that Americans are

Table 3.2 Americans' Perceptions of Their Own Tax Burden, 2019

	All Respondents	Democrats	Independents	Republicans
I pay too much	45%	39%	46%	50%
I pay the right amount	48	53	48	48
I pay too little	7	9	6	3
N	1,141	550	222	369

Source: YouGov survey, October 2019.

perhaps surprisingly willing to pay taxes as investments in public welfare and are proud to consider themselves "taxpayers" contributing to the broader society.[5]

Our own survey, building from the work of Larry Bartels and of William Claggett and Byron Schafer, also shows that broad dislike of taxes may not be the only reason for the high levels of support for tax expenditures.[6] We asked respondents a simple question: "Do you feel that you, personally, are asked to pay more than you should in federal income taxes, about the right amount, or less than you should?" The results (shown in table 3.2) show that while there is obviously not much support for individuals to pay more in federal taxes, there is not a groundswell of support for paying less either: a plurality of respondents said that they were currently paying "the right amount" in taxes. Interestingly, this question yielded no massive partisan divide: even about half of Republicans said that they were not being taxed too much.

Do the Wealthy Pay Too Little in Taxes?

If there is one group that the general public thinks is paying too little in taxes, however, it's the wealthy. We show this attitude in two ways. First, we replicate the earlier question ("Do you feel that you, personally, are asked to pay more than you should in federal income taxes, about the right amount, or less than you should?"), except that instead of asking respondents about their own tax burden, we ask them about the tax burden of "the wealthy" (see table 3.3). Nearly 60 percent of respondents thought that the wealthy pay too little in taxes. The partisan divides are a bit larger here, but even so, even half of Republicans thought that the wealthy pay too little.

Table 3.3 Americans' Perceptions of the Tax Burden of the Wealthy, 2019

	All Respondents	Democrats	Independents	Republicans
The wealthy pay too much	19%	11%	19%	25%
The wealthy pay the right amount	23	12	28	12
The wealthy pay too little	58	77	53	44
N	1,141	550	222	369

Source: YouGov survey, October 2019.

To get away from the "more" or "less" question wording, we also asked respondents to indicate what percentage of their income they thought wealthy individuals *did* pay in taxes, and what percentage they thought they *should* pay in taxes. Respondents were presented with a slider bar, ranging from 0 to 100, and asked to move it first to what they thought the actual total tax rate of the top 1 percent of income earners is, and then to what they thought that tax rate should be. Table 3.4 shows the mean and median responses to these questions, as well as the responses that fall into the 10th, 25th, 75th, and 90th percentiles. As might be expected, respondents were all over the map, both in what they thought the top 1 percent of income earners pay in taxes and in what they thought the wealthy should pay: some thought that the wealthy either do or should pay next to nothing in taxes, while others thought that tax rates for the wealthy are well above current norms, and should be. But in general, both mean and median responses centered on a rate that was modestly higher than the actual effective tax rate for the top 1 percent of earners of 26 percent, according to recent research from the Tax Policy Center.[7]

Importantly, the rate respondents thought that the top 1 percent should be paying was higher than the rate they thought that they were in fact paying (see table 3.5). The mean "preferred" tax rate was about seven percentage points higher than the mean "perceived" top tax rate, and the median preferred rate was about eleven points higher than the median perceived rate. When we compare responses to these two questions across individual respondents, we see that roughly two-thirds of respondents, according to this measure, thought that the wealthy should be paying more than they currently are, while only 20 percent thought

Table 3.4 Americans' Attitudes Toward the Tax Rates of the Top 1 Percent of Income Earners, 2019

	Mean	Tenth Percentile	Twenty-Fifth Percentile	Median	Seventy-Fifth Percentile	Ninetieth Percentile
Tax rate that respondents think the wealthy pay	33%	7%	14%	27%	50%	67%
Tax rate that respondents think the wealthy *should* pay	40	15	25	38	51	70

Source: YouGov survey, October 2019.

Table 3.5 Americans' Perceptions of the Tax Burden of the Top 1 Percent of Income Earners, by Party, 2019

	All Respondents	Democrats	Independents	Republicans
The wealthy pay too much in taxes	20%	9%	18%	36%
The wealthy pay too little in taxes	67	77	67	39
N	1,135	547	220	368

Source: YouGov survey, October 2019.

that they should be paying less. Even though Americans overstate the actual effective tax rate for wealthy earners, they by and large still think they should be paying more.

So even though the effect of programs like the Home Mortgage Interest Deduction is to lower the taxes of upper-income earners, a clear majority of Americans want the wealthy to pay more taxes, not less. This fits with other research regarding attitudes toward top income earners. Although Americans believe broadly in the idea of "meritocracy"—that hard work leads to success—there is a wealth of work showing that Americans, of all political stripes, are at best tolerant of inequality, may be somewhat resentful of wealthy Americans, and are likely to believe that income

Table 3.6 Americans' Perceptions of Where Social Benefits Accrue, 2019

	Mortgage Interest Deduction	Retirement Savings Tax Break	Public Health Spending	Social Security
Accrues primarily to upper-income citizens	49%	42%	17%	20%
Accrues primarily to middle-income citizens	43	52	19	50
Accrues primarily to lower-income citizens	8	6	65	30

Source: YouGov survey, October 2019.

earners in the top 1 percent are wealthy because of luck or circumstances of birth.[8]

Does the Public Know Who Benefits from Social Tax Expenditures?

It could be the case, then, that citizens are misinformed about the effects of certain tax expenditures; perhaps they think that programs like these benefit lower-income earners. This is a belief that makes sense, given the "submerged" delivery mechanism of such programs.[9] But at least as a general rule, the idea that the public does not know who these programs' beneficiaries are does not appear to explain the support for them as well.

We asked respondents who benefits (the wealthy, the middle class, or the poor) from four programs: two upwardly distributing tax expenditure programs (the mortgage interest deduction and the retirement savings tax credit) and two downwardly distributing public spending areas (public health and Social Security).[10] Data are presented in table 3.6.

As a whole, the public does understand the degree to which programs such as the mortgage interest credit benefit the wealthy. On balance, we see that the public sees a contrast between such programs and direct spending programs and understands, correctly, that the tax expenditures, unlike direct spending programs, do not distribute benefits downward.[11] These questions, of course, are imperfect—among other things, they cannot get at, for instance, how respondents define "upper-income earners." But it is clear that people can make a distinction between the redistributive consequences of tax expenditures and direct spending. Public ignorance of redistributive effects does not seem to tell the complete story of the broad support enjoyed by tax expenditure programs.

Factors Influencing Social Spending Attitudes

As we have noted, most public opinion research on social spending has focused on direct spending. This research has produced an excellent body of knowledge on the correlates of support for social spending programs. We build from that work here to develop a general model of public support for tax expenditure programs, focusing primarily on three factors: partisanship, values, and self-interest.

Partisanship

It is well known, of course, that citizens use broad dispositional factors such as partisanship to orient themselves to the political world and form opinions on important political issues. Partisanship functions as a heuristic tool, that is, as a place from which citizens can draw cues about the likely targets and effects of a policy and, increasingly, an affective orientation that can lead them to understand what "side" to take on a particular issue.[12] We see this clearly in both attitudes and elite behavior with respect to domestic spending programs.[13] If Republicans are advocating for a program while Democrats are opposing it, it is only natural for partisans to follow suit.

For Americans who base their support for government programs on ideological or partisan considerations, tax subsidies to promote social welfare present a predicament. When it comes to direct social spending in most domains, this heuristic provides a fairly clear way to understand policies— liberals want a government that does and spends more, while conservatives want a government that does and spends less. But social tax subsidy programs present conflicting informational cues as to whether the program in question is a conservative or liberal form of policymaking.

If a respondent focuses on the social policy or target group aspects of the program, rather than on the tax break information, they may lean toward categorizing the program as a liberal policy. However, if the social tax expenditure program is highlighted as a tax break or subsidy to the private sector—or attention is brought to the distributive effects of its benefits as a regressively structured program—then it may be better categorized as a conservative form of policymaking. In addition, since many kinds of social tax expenditures are supported (or opposed) by policymakers in ways that cut across ideological and partisan lines, following elite rhetoric may not provide as much useful information as elite rhetoric on direct spending. These crosscutting ideological signals create ambiguity for Americans trying to line up their policy preference in a way that fits with standard party cues.[14]

Self-interest

Research on the role of economic self-interest in American public opinion, particularly on spending issues, has reached a nuanced conclusion.[15] Individuals behaving in their own self-interest, as defined by Tammy Henderson and her colleagues, as a condition "where individuals seek to maximize the benefits and minimize the costs of the specific choices with which they are confronted," would seek to support policies that benefit them economically, while opposing policies that do not.[16] There is, of course, evidence that self-interest of this sort matters in American politics—low-income citizens tend to support more redistribution compared to upper-income citizens. For example, some studies show that citizens who qualify for a specific tax break are more supportive of the program.[17] But the effect of self-interest is often muted in Americans' political behavior, either because other concerns (such as partisanship) are more important or because citizens are ignorant about the likely effects of a policy on their economic well-being.

The structure of social tax expenditures, however, allows another, perhaps more direct avenue for self-interest to work in shaping attitudes toward programs. Rather than simply being generic public spending, these programs are targeted in direct and precise ways to encourage certain behaviors. Many major social tax subsidies are tied to company benefits. Workers who are offered and enroll in employment-based social programs are made aware of these benefits at the time of their hiring, and throughout the course of their employment, by human resource departments. The process of enrolling in these programs requires active participation that makes employees aware of the direct benefit they derive as citizens from doing so.[18]

For many other programs, citizens must enter information on their tax forms to claim tax breaks for mortgage interest, property tax payments, student loan interest, charitable contributions, and many more deductible expenses. Moreover, taxpayers usually enter this information for many consecutive years while they pay down their thirty-year mortgage, pay off their long-term student loan debt, deduct their annual contributions to a church, school, or other nonprofit, and so on. This process reminds citizens every year about which activities are associated with federal tax subsidies (homeownership, employment benefits, charitable contributions) and which are not. In other words, citizens, again, have to take active steps to claim such benefits. Annually filing a tax return may help remind citizens when a survey question is asked or a policy is discussed in the news that they benefit from that program. Self-interest of this narrow sort ("I use this program, so I like it") might be more relevant to support for tax expenditure programs.

As we noted earlier, scholars—most notably Suzanne Mettler—argue that many who use social tax expenditure programs do not think that they are benefiting from a "government social program."[19] But this does not necessarily mean that they are unaware of receiving some government aid, in some form, for taking the actions that they take. Here, we reexamine the claim that citizens who benefit from social tax expenditures are unaware of the role of government in providing them. In this survey, we asked a nationally representative sample of adults "whether or not they had benefited from a government subsidy program." This question is similar to the main survey question from the Mettler study, but we replaced "government social program" with the phrase "government subsidy program." Then, in a way similar to the Mettler study, we asked respondents if they had benefited from specific social tax expenditure and direct social spending programs.

Our results are reported in table 3.7, where we compare them to the results of the Mettler study.[20] First, the simple change in framing from "social" to "subsidy" reduced the percentage of social tax expenditure recipients who claimed that they had not benefited from the government. There were double-digit movements of beneficiaries toward recognizing the role of government in three education-related social tax expenditure programs (HOPE and Lifetime Learning Credits, 529 plans, and student loans). However, there was little change from their previous views on whether they had benefited from the Home Mortgage Interest Deduction and the Child Care Tax Credit. The framing change also affected recipients of direct spending social programs, who moved in the other

Table 3.7 Beneficiaries of Social Programs Who Reported That They Had Not Benefited from a Government Subsidy Program, 2019, Versus a Government Social Program, 2011

Program	Claimed Not to Have Used a Government Subsidy Program	Claimed Not to Have Used a Government Social Program (Mettler 2011)	Difference
Home Mortgage Interest Deduction	61.5%	60.0%	1.5%
Social Security	55.5	44.1	11.4
529 and Coverdell tax-deferred savings plans for college	53.7	64.3	–10.6
Child Care and Dependent Care Tax Credits	50.8	51.7	–0.9
HOPE and Lifetime Learning Credits	48.1	59.6	–11.5
Unemployment insurance	45.8	43.0	2.8
Obamacare	42.0	NA	NA
Student loans	39.8	53.3	–13.5
Medicaid	34.9	27.8	7.1

Source: YouGov survey, October 2019; Mettler 2011.

Note: N = 1,000. Social tax expenditures are in italics.

direction—reporting that they had not benefited from a "government subsidy." For example, Social Security and Medicare recipients were more likely to claim that they had not used a government program than in the 2011 survey.

By no means do these results, which are based on descriptive statistics from one survey question, present a definitive picture of the role of self-interest in constructing preferences for social tax expenditures. However, they do provide some evidence that changing the framing from "government social program" to "government subsidy" alters the perception among some social welfare recipients (of both direct and indirect programs) on whether or not they are beneficiaries of federal aid. And the fact that perceptions on this critical question can be manipulated so easily may call into question the validity of self-reports from citizens, who use different programs, on their reliance on the federal government for economic security. More broadly speaking, it stands to reason that people are aware of the tax breaks they receive, regardless of what they call them. We provide more systematic analysis of self-interest in the formation of attitudes toward spending in our general model, which follows later in the chapter.

Values

Research on opinions toward government spending also shows a pivotal role for political values. Broad values—abstract, general conceptions about the desirable and undesirable states of human life—matter to whether people are positively oriented toward government spending in general and toward spending on targeted programs in particular.[21]

In this chapter, we focus on two values known to be particularly important to support for social spending: egalitarianism and humanitarianism. Egalitarianism—belief in the general equality of all citizens—has been found to be significantly connected to support for a variety of social spending policies.[22] Egalitarians support government spending as a way to reduce opportunity and income gaps between rich and poor, and also as a way to provide social services as a matter of moral or legal obligation. Humanitarianism—defined by "the belief that people have responsibilities toward others and should come to the assistance of others in need"—also plays a role in support for social spending.[23]

Although these values are connected, they are conceptually different. Egalitarian values, in focusing on the issue of welfare as a social right, are based on the belief that citizens are entitled to a benefit or particular standard of living that meets their needs simply as a function of living in a good society.[24] Humanitarianism, by contrast, is less concerned with the broad idea of social rights as a concept and more focused on the importance of helping people struggling with particular problems or life situations.

Importantly, egalitarianism and humanitarianism generally lead to support for different kinds of social welfare policies. Egalitarianism naturally lends itself to support for broad-based interventions and programs designed to help those in need and to level the economic and social playing fields, broadly defined. Humanitarianism, by contrast, generates more support for policies that address the targeted needs or particular problems of limited sections of the population simply because it is the right thing to do.

Given these differences, we might expect these two values to have differing impacts on support for tax expenditure programs, which, by design, are targeted to specific sectors (such as low-income workers, or parents paying college tuition) in order to meet specific needs (making ends meet in a low-wage job, or sending a child to college). These programs do not, in other words, "redistribute wealth," generally speaking, but provide assistance to particular people in particular situations. We might thus expect humanitarian values to be strongly connected to support for tax expenditure programs, particularly downwardly distributing ones. It is more difficult, however, to see the impact of such values on attitudes toward upwardly distributing tax expenditure programs. Humanitarianism is meant to signal support for people in need, so its impact on these programs, even though they help people achieve targeted goals, is likely to be smaller.[25]

Modeling Support for Tax Expenditure Programs

In what follows, we estimate a series of models, using indicators of the factors influencing social spending attitudes discussed in the previous section, to model the correlates of support for tax expenditure programs. The dependent variables in the models are the five-point scales of attitudes toward the seven tax expenditure programs noted earlier. We model these attitudes as a function of partisanship and through measures of "self-interest" capturing experiences with each of the programs, indicators of egalitarian and humanitarian values, and a battery of standard sociodemographic predictors. Partisanship is measured using a standard seven-point Democrat-Republican scale.

To measure self-interest, we asked respondents about their activities or a personal status that would indicate their eligibility for or experience with a particular social tax expenditure program. Specifically, respondents were asked if they currently purchased health insurance through their employer (health care tax credit), contributed to an employer-sponsored retirement plan (retirement savings credit), owned a home or condo (mortgage interest deduction), paid college tuition for themselves or a dependent (tuition credit), were paying off student loans (student loan credit), or were paying for day care for a child or other dependent (dependent day care credit).[26] While respondents who experienced these situations may not necessarily have been using these tax expenditures (for example, if they owned a completely paid-off home, they would be ineligible for the mortgage interest tax credit), these indicators strongly suggest that respondents were benefiting from the relevant tax subsidy in their own lives.[27]

Our indicators of values are two truncated scales of standard egalitarianism and humanitarianism.[28] Egalitarianism is measured by asking respondents to rate their level of agreement or disagreement (on a five-point scale) with the following two statements: "Incomes should be more equal because every family's needs for food, housing, and so on, are the same," and "This country would be better off if we worried less about how equal people are" (reverse-coded). Humanitarianism is measured through level of agreement with these two statements: "One should always find ways to help those less fortunate than oneself," and "It is better not to be too kind to people, since that kindness can often be abused" (reverse-coded). To these indicators we add measures of age, family income (measured on a fifteen-point scale), gender, and race.

Table 3.8 shows the results of regression models predicting support for each of the seven programs. Standardized coefficients are presented here, to give a sense of the relative magnitude of the effects of each variable. The first thing to note in the models is that partisan identification is generally unpredictive of attitudes toward these issues. For only two of the tax expenditures is partisanship a significant predictor of support. Table 3.9 provides a cleaner look at partisan differences in support for these programs and again illustrates that partisan divides are small or nonexistent for many tax expenditure programs. This is especially true for the three most upwardly distributing programs: Democrats and Republicans support the health care and retirement tax credits and the mortgage interest deduction at essentially identical rates.

Partisanship still matters when it comes to the wage assistance program: Republicans remain less likely to support a low-wage subsidy than Democrats. This, of course, fits with what is known about party divides on redistribution. But even here, the partisan differences are relatively muted compared to direct spending on a program like welfare: in the 2016 Cooperative Congressional Election Study (CCES), the difference between the percentage of Democrats and Republicans who wanted to "spend less" on welfare was more than forty points.

The values indicators generally behave as expected: neither egalitarianism nor humanitarianism matter to support for the three most upwardly distributing tax expenditures, but both consistently matter to predicting support for low-wage assistance, tuition credits, student loan interest, and the dependent care credit. There was little evidence, however, for our hypothesis that humanitarianism would matter more to support for tax expenditure programs.

Table 3.8 Americans' Attitudes Toward Social Tax Subsidies, 2019

Independent Variable	Health Care	Retirement	Mortgage Interest	Low-Income Wage Assistance	Tuition Credits	Student Loans	Dependent Day Care Credits
Party identification	-.04	.00	-.01	-.12*	-.00	-.01	-.11*
Egalitarianism	-.04	.00	-.01	.28*	.10*	.17*	.10*
Humanitarianism	.10*	.06	.03	.08*	.07*	.05*	.14*
Race (white)	.13*	.04	-.03	.01	-.01	.02	.04
Gender (female)	.02	.00	.01	.02	.00	.02	.02
Age	-.00	-.00	-.00	-.06+	-.10*	-.07*	.02
Income	.11*	.11*	-.00	-.07*	.04	.01+	.05
Health insurance through employer	.07*						
Retirement savings through employer		.09*					
Owns home/condo			.06*				
Currently paying tuition					.06+		
Has student loans						.15*	
Pays for dependent care							.02
R^2	.06	.03	.02	.11	.06	.10	.07
N	852	852	852	852	852	852	852

Source: YouGov survey, October 2019.

Note: Table entries are standardized regression coefficients.

$*p < .05; +p < .10$

Table 3.9 Americans' Support for Tax Expenditure Programs, by Party, 2019

	Democrats	Independents	Republicans	Net Difference Between Democrats and Republicans
Health care contributions	73%	74%	73%	0%
Retirement credit	71	70	71	0
Mortgage interest	62	59	61	1
Low-wage income assistance	70	53	45	25
Tuition credits	61	52	56	5
Student loan interest	67	52	51	16
Dependent care credit	72	60	56	16

Source: YouGov survey, October 2019.

Most interestingly, however, respondents' experience with tax expenditure programs was a consistent predictor of support for them: those who owned a home were significantly more likely to support the mortgage interest deduction than those who did not, those who had student loan debt were more likely to support the student loan tax credit, and so on.[29] These effects remain after controlling for income, race, and other factors that might lead someone to support or oppose such credits. That a person's experience using a program matters to supporting it is a wholly intuitive finding. But it also shows that these programs may not be as "hidden" as we thought: at least at the level of the individual user, people know which programs they benefit from and are more likely to express their support accordingly.

Conclusion: The Broad-Based Appeal of Tax Expenditures

Taken together, these models show that attitudes toward social tax expenditures are constructed differently than attitudes toward direct spending. In particular, powerful heuristics, such as partisanship, lose much of their value when talking about tax expenditures. To be sure, when it comes to determinants of public support, tax expenditures have many things in common with direct spending. Standard indicators of political and social values predict support for many direct spending programs; we see here that they matter for attitudes toward tax expenditures as well. Support for some direct spending programs has at least a modest self-interest compo-nent, and we see that self-interest also matters, perhaps in a more precise and targeted way, for support for tax expenditure programs.

In general, however, what stands out about these models is their rela-tive *lack* of fit to the data. Tax expenditures are not only popular—they are broadly popular. The typical kinds of partisan or other heuristic cues that help citizens decide whether to support or oppose particular direct spend-ing programs are not as prominent in public discussion of tax expenditure programs, rendering the differences in support for such programs across party or demographic lines muted or nonexistent. This is particularly true even when the distributive implications of such programs might lead to partisan or class polarization. Democrats, for example, tend to support upwardly distributing programs at roughly the same rate as Republicans. And while Republicans are not as supportive as Democrats of downwardly distributing ones, their opposition is muted when compared to their atti-tudes toward targeted direct spending programs (welfare or the Affordable Care Act, for example).

Our analysis shows that Americans who qualify for social tax expendi-tures report higher levels of support for these programs. We are not argu-ing that Americans who receive social tax subsidies view these programs as welfare; it is clear from other work that they do not see the benefits that way.[30] However, while the process of passing a tax expenditure program may seem hidden or shadowed, Americans who qualify for a subsidy program are clear about where in the tax code their federal benefits lie and favor this type of federal social spending.

We are thus left to explain the broad-based popularity of these programs, and why citizens support programs that, at least at first glance, may seem to violate their other core political principles. To do so we turn to a more precise examination of differences in how direct spending programs and tax expenditure programs are delivered, and the effect of the delivery mecha-nism itself on patterns of public support.

CHAPTER 4

Tax Expenditures and Direct Spending: A Comparison

IN CHAPTER 3, we examined patterns of support for tax expenditure programs and found that all of the country's major tax expenditure programs enjoyed majority or supermajority support, and that this support by and large extended across many lines of political difference. It also extended to programs that had many different kinds of distributive effects and helped many different types of populations. Chapter 3 left some questions unanswered, in particular the question of how the popularity of tax expenditure programs compares to attitudes toward direct spending programs. We know, for example, that programs such as Social Security and Medicare are also very popular, and that there is at least some reservoir of support for direct government assistance to the poor and other marginalized groups.

In this chapter, we look at both sides of the divided welfare state in order to understand not just patterns of support for social spending but also preferences for how such spending should be conducted. In particular, we more directly compare preferences for tax expenditures with preferences for direct spending. A wide variety of research suggests that spending on social policy goals is generally popular—the public is largely supportive of public efforts to improve education, assist the poor, improve infrastructure, and so on. This support usually remains strong even when people are reminded that such spending will cost tax money or interfere in some ways with private markets. But broad support for social spending faces a considerable counterweight—public dislike and distrust of the government entrusted to do that spending. A public that wants government to do and spend more in the abstract, in other words, sees significant practical barriers to government spending money efficiently and effectively.

We take an experimental approach to understanding preferences for both direct and indirect social spending, focusing on differences in how citizens view government spending done through direct appropriations and spending done through tax expenditures. Our goal is to see how support for the exact same social programs changes when the *delivery mechanism* of those programs (direct spending or tax expenditures) changes. We find that even when holding the cost, goals, and likely outcomes of a wide variety of social policies constant, citizens would like to see benefits delivered, all else being equal, through the tax code rather than through direct government programs.

Tax expenditures, because of how they deliver benefits, may provide a preferable way for government to spend money on social policy goals. Because tax expenditures are delivered privately, and in a way that does not connote "government spending" in the minds of citizens, they can provide the same kinds of social benefits as direct spending without invoking the specter of "big government" or government spending. This is especially true among people who might be especially prone to reject a large government role in shaping social policy, either for ideological reasons or simply because they distrust government.

Public Attitudes Toward Government and Government Spending

The American public has long been of two minds regarding its preference for the role of government in society. This distinction is often framed as one between *operational* liberalism and *symbolic* conservatism. When it comes to specific social policies (the operational side of public opinion), citizens generally want government to do and spend more; when they are asked about their preferences for government spending in nearly every major policy domain, the plurality response is "more spending."[1] But at the same time, citizens are more likely to identify symbolically as conservatives rather than liberals, they often express an abstract preference for a smaller and leaner government, and they reject labels that connote a preference for a larger, more activist government.[2]

These differences between abstract support for smaller government and programmatic support for a government that does more and spends more has led to a number of well-recognized disconnects in American public opinion, including the public's tendency to prefer abstract "conservative" ideals and values (for example, limited government, individualism, and belief in "meritocracy" and the idea that hard work and personal responsibility are integral to success) while supporting mostly "liberal" policy positions on issues of, for example, taxation, redistribution, and regulation.[3] This "conflicted conservatism" leads many segments of the American public to evaluate the worth of social programs through two different lenses: one that evaluates the benefits provided by programs, and one that evaluates the government or agency providing them.[4]

The distinction between "operationally liberal" and "symbolically conservative" implies certain things about American public opinion. The operationally liberal side supports the kinds of social policy goals that government is trying to achieve: citizens often support greater spending on social programs in part because they see value in the ends promised—better education, retirement security, and the like.[5] In fact, in the abstract Americans are often willing to pay more to solve such problems, even if they themselves are not the direct beneficiaries.[6]

But at the same time, the symbolically conservative side explains the public's long-standing skepticism toward "government intervention" in the market economy.[7] People might be willing to spend the money to address particular issues, but they also see this goal as conflicting with their broader individualistic orientations.[8] More importantly, Americans are often unable to trust government to spend money efficiently or effectively.[9]

The important point is this: when citizens are asked to think about the specific social problems that government is expected to solve, they tend to support more government spending. But when they are asked to think about whether they trust government to deliver benefits efficiently and effectively, or whether they support a "bigger government role" more abstractly defined, they support less spending. William Jacoby's analysis, for example, finds a wide disconnect between the number of Americans who say that they wish government to "spend less and offer fewer services" in the abstract and the number of those who wish to cut support for specific government programs.[10] Subsequent analyses and surveys by the CCES in 2014, the American National Election Study (ANES) in 2016, and many others support this point: support for cutting government spending is high in the abstract, but the only programs that generally garner anywhere near majority support for being cut are relatively minor ones (foreign aid, the arts), which comprise a tiny fraction of the federal budget.

This distinction is why the generally high levels of support for social spending as revealed in many national surveys might be taken as expressions of "soft support."[11] Take the standard battery of General Social Survey questions used in a massive body of research on social spending preferences. GSS questions are prefaced as follows: "We are faced with many problems in this country, none of which can be solved easily or inexpensively. I'm going to name some of these problems, and for each one I'd like you to tell me whether you think we're spending too much money on it, too little money, or about the right amount." Then respondents are simply read a list of programmatic areas—public health, education, national defense, and the like. These questions are widely used because they effectively ask about citizens' preferences in a number of programmatic domains at a level of abstraction that is likely to be meaningful to them.[12] But these questions do little to remind respondents that it is some form of "government" doing the spending. The GSS has experimented with versions of these questions that remind respondents that tax increases might be used to pay for this spending, but they still do not prime "government" explicitly.

Tax Expenditures and "Threading the Needle"

Given this distinction between abstract opposition and programmatic support for government intervention in a variety of domains, the public policy literature provides reason to think that citizens view direct social spending and social tax expenditure programs differently. Christopher Howard argues that policymakers turn to tax expenditures as a way to "thread the political needle" of funding popular social goals while seemingly advancing the virtues of individual initiative and smaller government.[13]

Social tax expenditures deliver benefits indirectly through the actions of private individuals and markets. Those who worry about the upwardly redistributing nature of many prominent tax expenditures often frame this lack of direct government action as a problem. Jacob Hacker, for example, refers to the policy process that creates tax expenditures as "subterranean," since tax expenditures are created outside the formal budget process and the administration of benefits is activated through a complex mix of public and private actors.[14] The resulting low visibility of tax expenditures makes it difficult for citizens to understand what this sort of social policy does and what effects it has.

Mettler, for example, shows that most citizens who receive social benefits through the tax code are unaware that they are even receiving government social benefits.[15] She finds that a majority of respondents who claimed to have used a tax expenditure program (such as the mortgage interest deduction or the child care credit) also claimed to have never benefited from a federal social program. Recipients of direct spending programs, by contrast, were more likely to acknowledge that they had used a government program and that the government had helped them in a time of need. The implication is that tax expenditure programs, though they provide government-directed benefits to citizens, are not viewed as "government programs" in the same way as programs financed through direct appropriations.

The relative lack of transparency of social tax expenditure programs has another important feature: it leads citizens to view them as "government actions" rather than as tax expenditure programs. Benefits distributed through tax expenditures are often not perceived, even by recipients of such benefits, as being government-provided. This implies that citizens do not necessarily view tax expenditures as an explicit government-based effort to intervene in social outcomes, nor do they view beneficiaries of tax expenditure programs as recipients of "government assistance"; instead, they view tax expenditures as ways through which citizens "help themselves" and save on their taxes.[16] Thus, a tax expenditure program is less likely than a direct spending program to be viewed through the abstract prism of "government" and "government spending"—with all of the negative connotations that those phrases evoke.

Social tax expenditures, then, comport better than direct spending with the dualistic tension between symbolic and operational political preferences. Operationally, they can address what the public perceives as important social problems by providing benefits to help individuals in certain situations and life circumstances. But social tax expenditures also comport well with a general lack of trust in government, abstract support for free markets, and demands for a smaller direct government role in managing the economy. At least in the abstract, tax expenditures can be delivered in a way that satisfies popular demand for particular forms of social spending while avoiding the "government spending" framing that citizens dislike and distrust. In other words, the design and delivery mechanism of particular public policies—more specifically, whether they are delivered through direct or indirect means—seem to be important determinants of whether citizens respond positively to them.

The Popularity of Direct Spending and Tax Expenditures: An Experimental Approach

Our basic expectations are straightforward. All else being equal, a program portrayed as providing tax credits from the government to individuals for engaging in particular behaviors will be received more positively by the public than one portrayed as providing direct payments from the government to the same individuals for the same behaviors. Of course, in the real world, not all is equal. Though, as we have discussed, tax expenditures generally seek to solve the same sorts of problems that direct expenditures aim to solve, they do so with different cost structures, different rewards, and different target beneficiaries. Preferences for employer-sponsored retirement plans are fundamentally different from preferences for government-administered pension plans such as Social Security. So to test the impact of the delivery mechanism itself, we turn to experimental analysis.

In what follows, we develop a set of experimental vignettes that will allow us to view the effects of the delivery mechanism itself on support for social policies above and beyond their cost and targeted beneficiaries. These experiments take six sets of social policies, with defined costs, defined targets, and defined behaviors that they wish to reward, and vary the mechanism through which the programs are delivered. The goal is to hold all aspects of a social policy constant, save for the means through which beneficiaries will receive benefits. The six policy areas are encouraging homeownership (by subsidizing mortgage interest payments), saving for retirement, paying for basic necessities, repaying student loans, purchasing health insurance, and encouraging "green" energy consumption.

For each policy, respondents were randomly assigned to either a "tax expenditure" frame, in which the benefit is delivered through tax credits, or a "direct spending" frame, in which the benefit is delivered through direct government expenditures.[17] Using a 0–4 scale, we then asked respondents whether they "strongly oppose," "oppose," "neither support nor oppose," "support," or "strongly support" each program. The experimental vignettes were:

Mortgage Interest

Tax expenditure: "Some have endorsed a program that would provide individuals and families assistance in making the monthly payments on their homes. Under this program, citizens who earn taxable income would be allowed to deduct their mortgage interest payments from their taxable income. These tax credits would reduce the amount of taxes that homeowners must pay to the federal government, thus increasing the amount of money they have to make their mortgage payments. The total cost of this program, in terms of lost federal government tax revenue, is expected to be about $100 billion per year."

Direct spending: "Some have endorsed a program that would provide individuals and families assistance in making the monthly payments on their homes. Under this program, citizens would receive annual grants from the federal government to help offset the amount of money they pay in interest on their mortgage. The total cost of this program, in terms of federal government spending, is expected to be about $100 billion per year."

Saving for Retirement

Tax expenditure: "Some have endorsed a program that would assist individuals in saving for retirement while still paying day-to-day bills. Under this plan, individuals who earn taxable income and invest money in a private retirement plan would be able to deduct the amount that they save for retirement from their taxable income. This tax credit would reduce the amount of taxes that workers must pay to the federal government. The total cost of this program is expected to be roughly $115 billion per year."

Direct spending: "Some have endorsed a program that would assist individuals in saving for retirement while still paying day-to-day bills. Under this plan, individuals who invest money in a private retirement plan would be eligible for government payments that would help offset the amount of money that they save for retirement. The total cost of this program is expected to be roughly $115 billion per year."

Paying for Necessities

Tax expenditure: "Some have endorsed a program that would provide low-income citizens with assistance in paying for groceries and other necessities. Under this program, citizens who earn taxable income would be eligible to deduct the amount of money that they pay for groceries from their taxable income. These tax credits would reduce the amount of federal income tax that these citizens pay each year and could result in a citizen receiving a tax credit from the federal government instead of paying federal income taxes at all. The total cost of this program is expected to be $65 billion per year."

Direct spending: "Some have endorsed a program that would provide low-income citizens with assistance in paying for groceries and other necessities. Under this program, certain citizens would receive monthly checks from the government that could be used to purchase groceries and other necessities. The total cost of this program is expected to be $65 billion per year."

Paying Off Student Loans

Tax expenditure: "Some have endorsed a program that would provide college graduates with assistance in making their student loan payments. Under this program, individuals with student loan debt would be eligible for tax credits that would partially offset the amount of money that they pay in student loans each year. These tax credits would reduce the amount of money that borrowers must pay to the federal government in income tax. The total cost of this program is expected to be roughly $30 billion per year."

Direct spending: "Some have endorsed a program that would provide college graduates with assistance in making their student loan payments. Under this program, individuals with student loan debt would be eligible for cash payments from the federal government that would partially offset the amount of money that they pay in student loans each year. The total cost of this program is expected to be roughly $30 billion per year."

Purchasing Health Insurance

Tax expenditure: "Some have endorsed a program designed to help individuals pay for health insurance. Under this program, individuals who participate in health insurance plans through their employer will be permitted to deduct the amount of money that they pay for their insurance from their taxable income, thus reducing the amount of tax that they must pay to the federal government. The total cost of this program is expected to be $150 billion per year."

Direct spending: "Some have endorsed a program designed to help individuals pay for health insurance. Under this program, individuals who participate in health insurance plans through their employer will be eligible for government grants that will help offset the amount that they pay for this insurance. The total cost of this program is expected to be $150 billion per year."

Encouraging "Green" Energy Consumption

Tax expenditure: "Some policymakers have endorsed a program that would assist individuals in paying for 'green' improvements—such as the installation of solar panels or high-efficiency heating systems—to their homes. Families who completed such improvements would be able to use tax breaks to deduct some of their costs from their federal tax bill. The cost of this program, in terms of lost revenue to the federal government, is expected to be roughly $10 billion per year."

Direct spending: "Some policymakers have endorsed a program that would assist individuals in paying for 'green' improvements—such as the installation of solar panels or high-efficiency heating systems— to their homes. Families who completed such improvements would be able to receive checks from the federal government to reimburse them for some of their costs. The cost of this program is expected to be roughly $10 billion per year."

Results

As would be expected given the varying nature of the programs, top-line support varied based on characteristics of the programs themselves. These differences reflect all of the other factors that enter into understanding the public's level of support for various social policies: the beneficiaries, the likely cost, the social goal being pursued, and so on.

At the individual level, there is also evidence that support for each of these programs varies in predictable ways across the factors known to affect social spending attitudes: Republicans, conservatives, individualists, and (to a lesser extent) whites are generally less favorable to social spending. These results suggest that attitudes toward these issues are predictable in ways that one would expect given past research on the determinants of social spending preferences.[18] They also confirm that, despite the unconventional wording of our vignettes, respondents were viewing these programs through the same lens through which they viewed other questions on similar policies.

Nevertheless, we also have strong evidence that the way in which a benefit is delivered has a marked impact on public support. Table 4.1 provides cross-tabulations of support by program and delivery frame, and table 4.2 shows mean levels of support for each program. For five of the six programs (all but "paying for necessities"), we see that support is higher when the program is delivered through the tax code rather than through direct spending.

The effects of the delivery mechanism are strongest for the "mortgage interest" and "saving for retirement" questions: in both cases, mean support for the policies decreased by more than 25 percent when the programs were portrayed as cash payments to homeowners (or savers) rather than as tax advantages to homeowners (or savers), and in both cases the delivery mechanism was the difference between whether a program received plurality support or plurality opposition. These programs as currently constituted, it is worth noting, are two of the most upwardly distributing tax expenditures in the federal tax code. Though we did not test this proposition directly, it is at least possible that Americans have an especially high tolerance for redistributing upward through the tax code money that they would not have if benefits were delivered through cash payments.[19] The effects were smaller, but still meaningful, for the student loan, health insurance, and green energy programs: in all cases, respondents liked the program more if its benefits were delivered indirectly.[20]

The "paying for necessities" program—the most sharply downwardly distributing program on our list—was the only one for which support was roughly equal across frames. There are several reasons why this may be the case; one likely possibility is that attitudes toward welfare-like programs are shaped so strongly by perceptions of the beneficiaries themselves that there was simply less room for delivery mechanism to matter in this sort of

Table 4.1 Americans' Support for Social Programs, by Spending Mode, 2015

	Mortgage Interest		Retirement Savings		Paying for Necessities	
	Direct Spending	Tax Expenditure	Direct Spending	Tax Expenditure	Direct Spending	Tax Expenditure
Strongly oppose/oppose	44%	30%	36%	17%	26%	26%
Neither support nor oppose	24	25	30	27	19	19
Strongly support/support	32	45	33	56	55	55
N	499	495	502	492	481	517
Strongly oppose/oppose	44%	30%	36%	17%	26%	26%
Neither support nor oppose	24	25	30	27	19	19
Strongly support/support	32	45	33	56	55	55
N	499	495	502	492	481	517

	Student Loans		Paying for Health Care		Green Energy Credits	
	Direct Spending	Tax Expenditure	Direct Spending	Tax Expenditure	Direct Spending	Tax Expenditure
Strongly oppose/oppose	33%	22%	28%	17%	29%	26%
Neither support nor oppose	21	21	22	24	27	25
Strongly support/support	46	57	50	58	45	49
N	492	506	458	537	589	607

Source: YouGov survey, August 2015.

Table 4.2 Americans' Mean Levels of Support for Social Policy Programs, by Spending Mode, 2015

	Direct Spending	Tax Expenditure	N
Mortgage interest	1.78	2.23*	994
Retirement savings	1.94	2.59*	994
Paying for necessities	2.44	2.45	998
Student loan interest	2.19	2.54*	998
Paying for health care	2.26	2.59*	995
Green energy credits	2.20	2.30	1,196

Source: YouGov survey, August 2015.

Note: * = mean differences between spending mode frames is significant at the .05 level.

generic policy frame.[21] We address the role that delivery mechanism may play in shaping perceptions of beneficiaries more fully in chapter 5.

Who Cares About Delivery Mechanism? The Role of Ideology and Trust

So far we have basic evidence that benefits delivered through the tax code are more popular than otherwise identical benefits delivered through direct means—because tax expenditures, we hypothesize, do not prime the idea of "government" and all of its negative connotations in the way that direct spending does. Thus, not only does the delivery mechanism matter to a social program's popularity, but the delivery mechanism is especially important for people who are otherwise opposed to the principle of government spending or skeptical about the government's ability to solve social problems. In what follows, we isolate two variables that might help us better understand why delivery mechanism matters, and for whom it matters most.

Political Ideology: Principled Opposition to Government Spending

We know that while the terms "liberal" and "conservative" are multifaceted, encompass various dimensions of belief, and are often misunderstood by large segments of the public, the two ideologies do provide a way of understanding individuals' core orientations to the social world. They connote very different views of the proper role and scope of government in remediating social inequality and of the role of government more generally.

Conservatism's core principles are that market forces do more good than harm, and that societies with strong and free markets ultimately are more prosperous than societies in which government tries to reduce income differences or provide for those who cannot or will not provide for themselves.[22]

On balance, conservatives are tolerant of government efforts to redistribute wealth downward.[23] But they are also more strongly opposed than others to governmental intervention in the economy, and more than liberals, they strongly prize economic individualism as a core political value.[24] To the extent that government should get involved, in other words, conservatives believe that it should focus on helping people who are also helping themselves. Just as importantly, even conservatives who are worried about issues like income inequality are generally unconvinced that government can address such issues effectively without introducing additional problems of its own.[25]

Though economic liberals in the United States are not exactly "pro-government," they are typically more receptive to the idea that markets can fail to deliver certain kinds of desired outcomes, and thus they are more supportive of government efforts to help poor citizens and groups. They react less negatively to the idea of "activist government," at least in the economic sphere. Liberals in the United States still embrace some values of economic individualism, but they balance such ideals with a commitment to some form of equality as an ideal and some form of government intervention to help achieve that ideal.[26] Liberals are more ambivalent than conservatives toward the balance of power between government and private markets: they are more egalitarian, but also abstractly share with conservatives an endorsement of the role of individual effort and initiative in shaping success.[27]

These stylized philosophies suggest that liberals and conservatives will react differently to the means through which a social benefit is delivered. For conservatives, we expect that the portrayal of a program as either direct spending or a tax expenditure will have a substantial impact on their support. Even if tax expenditures are the same as direct spending in cost and intent, it is easier to view what is perceived as a decrease in the amount of an individual's own tax burden as a reward for individual initiative and effort (not as "government assistance"), compared with direct spending—a direct payment from the government to the individual. For liberals, the reverse is likely to be true: how a program is portrayed (as financed through either

Table 4.3 Americans' Trust in Government, 2015

"How often do you think that you can trust the government to do what is right?"	All Respondents	Liberals	Moderates	Conservatives
Just about always	4%	3%	2%	2%
Most of the time	13	21	17	6
Only some of the time	47	56	47	38
Almost never	36	20	34	55

Source: YouGov survey, August 2015.

direct spending or tax expenditures) should matter less for them, given liberals' greater levels of abstract support for activist (that is, direct) solutions to social problems and greater tolerance for ceding control over government in solving those problems.

Trust in Government: "Practical" Opposition to Government Spending

Americans' trust in the federal government is low and, by most accounts, getting steadily lower over time. Fewer than one-quarter of Americans trust the government to do what is right just about always or most of the time, down from historic highs of roughly 70 percent during the Eisenhower and Kennedy eras and roughly 50 percent near the end of Bill Clinton's second term.[28] Table 4.3, taken from a question on our 2015 survey, shows levels of trust in government both overall and by political ideology. Although, as would be expected (especially when a Democrat was in the White House), liberals trusted the government more than conservatives did, trust was not particularly high among any ideological group.

Political trust as (following Marc Hetherington) "the degree to which people perceive that government is producing outcomes consistent with their expectations" is a substantively important predictor of citizen support for a variety of policy initiatives.[29] This is particularly true when it comes to government spending, which requires that citizens pay some cost if government-provided social benefits and services are to be funded. Above and beyond party, ideology, or other factors, citizens who do not believe that government will carry out its goals efficiently or effectively, or who perceive the designers of policy as unworthy of their confidence or as unlikely to implement policy in a way consistent with their promises, tend to be less willing to pay the cost of additional spending. Trust, in the words of Thomas Rudolph and Jillian Evans, thus operates as a "simple heuristic that helps citizens decide whether to support or oppose government spending in a particular policy domain."[30] Hetherington notes that this is particularly true when citizens are being implicitly asked to make material sacrifices to support more government spending—that is, to support spending on programs (such as for public schooling, higher education, aid to the poor, or public health) that might redistribute wealth away from themselves in an effort to reduce inequality or increase equality of opportunity.[31]

The impact of trust is strong even when citizens agree that there are social problems that cannot be solved through market forces alone: a lack of belief in markets or business to solve problems does not necessarily translate into greater support for government intervention if citizens do not trust government to intervene properly.[32] Hetherington and Rudolph, for example, find that support for downwardly distributing economic stimulus spending in response to the Great Recession of 2007 to 2009 was strongly conditioned by political trust, even after controlling for partisanship, ideology, and other factors.[33]

Just as with those opposed to "big government" on principle, then, those who do not trust the government to do a good job at spending money or solving problems might be particularly apt to view tax expenditures as a more palatable way to solve social problems: because tax expenditures ultimately rely on private citizens, businesses, and markets to distribute benefits, they should steer citizens away from thinking about the distribution of such benefits from an institution that they think will fail to deliver them. Tax expenditure spending, in other words, should be less likely to activate the "trust heuristic" that leads citizens to evaluate spending programs through the lens of political trust.

The Interaction of Ideology and Trust

Rudolph and Evans note that the impact of trust on spending preferences is greater for conservatives than it is for liberals, since conservatives (unlike liberals) have to "sacrifice" ideological principles to support more government activity in various domains.[34] For conservatives, supporting government spending in a particular domain means espousing a position that cuts against their ideological disposition. Conservatives thus rely more on trust when deciding whether an increase in direct spending in a particular domain is warranted, since trusting government is a more necessary condition for supporting greater spending to which their ideological principles say they "should" be opposed. But tax expenditures—again, because they rely on private markets to handle the final distribution of preferences— are more palatable to conservative ideological principles because less ideological sacrifice is required to support them. We thus expect that the impact of spending mode on the relevance of trust will be stronger for self-identified conservatives, who prefer market solutions to centralized ones and for whom limited government is generally more of a prized virtue than it is for other citizens.

For liberals, the impact of spending mode on the relevance of trust should be weaker, as liberals need not make as great an ideological sacrifice to support direct spending as conservatives do. Although we expect trust to still matter to the social spending of liberals, their preferences should, in general, be less driven by how money is spent and more by the sorts of problems money is used to address.

Analyses: Ideology and Trust

In sum, then, our expectations are threefold. First, we expect that the impact of delivery mechanism on support for social policy will be greater for conservatives than for liberals. Second, we expect an individual's level of political trust to be greater for direct spending programs than for tax expenditure programs. Finally, the impact of spending mode on the relevance of trust should be greater for conservatives than for liberals.

To begin, we take a basic look at how the spending frame might differentially affect liberal and conservative attitudes toward social policy. Figure 4.1 illustrates self-identified liberal and conservative means of support by spending frame for each of the six social policies. The data show a clear pattern: spending frame matters more to program support for conservatives than it does for liberals, and framing a program as a tax expenditure does substantially more to increase support for it among conservatives than among liberals.

The results are clearest for the mortgage interest and retirement security programs. Both of these programs are deeply unpopular among Republicans

Figure 4.1 Mean Levels of Social Program Support, by Spending Frame and Ideology, 2015

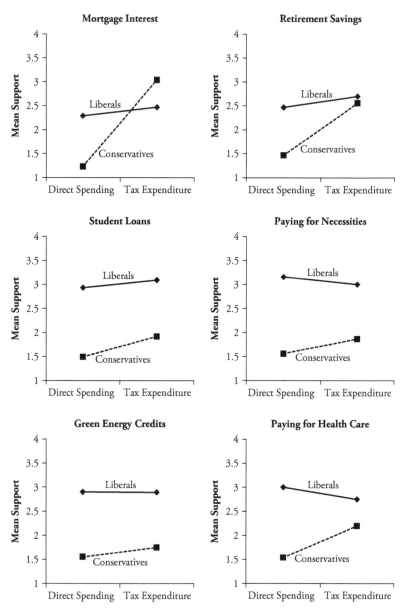

Source: YouGov survey, August 2015.

when framed as direct spending. But when framed as tax credits, support increases substantially: by 16 percent on the 0–4 scale for the retirement savings program, and by nearly 50 percent for the mortgage interest program. Meanwhile, we see only very modest (and not statistically significant) increases in support among liberals for these programs when they are framed as tax expenditures. Liberals' support for or opposition to these programs seems to be grounded in factors unrelated to how they are delivered. For conservatives, the opposite is true: delivering subsidies for homeownership or retirement through direct spending is deeply unpopular, but delivering the same subsidies through the tax code is quite popular.

The results are similar, though less stark, for the student loan program. The mean difference in conservative support across framing conditions (0.43) is more than twice as much as the mean difference in liberal support across conditions (0.19). The results for the other three programs show at least modest evidence, in the bivariate context, for program delivery mechanism to have differential effects on liberals and conservatives. For conservatives, support for programs to help people pay for necessities, health care, and green energy increased when the program was delivered through the tax code. But for liberals, support for all three programs decreased when framed as a tax expenditure (though the mean difference in framing conditions is statistically significant only for the health care policy).

The central message from these basic analyses is that conservatives are more receptive to social programs that are delivered through the tax code than programs delivered through direct spending. Consistent with our expectations, conservatives, who are generally opposed to government intervention in the economy, are more likely to reject out of hand programs that call for a direct expansion of government. If these same programs are delivered through the tax code, the possibility of conservative acceptance of them increases, even if they ultimately cost as much as direct spending programs.

Simply relying on tax expenditures as the spending mode, however, is not necessarily enough to overcome other sources of conservative opposition to certain programs. (Though green energy subsidies were more popular among conservatives when delivered through the tax code, conservatives were not particularly apt to support these subsidies in either framing condition.) But using tax subsidies as the delivery mechanism removes at least one source of resistance to such programs. Liberals, who are more concerned about what a program does than about how it is delivered, tend to not care as much about spending mode.

Figure 4.2 illustrates a similar set of results segmenting the population by levels of political trust. For purposes of this analysis, we segmented respondents into "low trust" (the 36 percent of the 2015 sample who said that they trusted the government "almost never") and "high trust" (the 17 percent of the sample who trusted the government "most of the time" or "just about always").[35] As would be expected given the high levels of correlation between ideology and trust, there is a good deal of similarity between the results for ideology and these figures. Again, however, we see evidence that spending frame is more relevant to the views of those with low trust in government than to the views of those with high trust.

Table 4.4 examines the roles of trust and ideology in the multivariate context. This table presents results of regression models predicting attitudes toward each of the six policies by spending frame, as a function of trust (measured using the five-point scale described earlier), ideology (using a 1–5 liberal-conservative scale), and using a basic battery of sociodemographic covariates. The models for each policy area are estimated using seemingly unrelated estimation, which allows us to test whether coefficient estimates for any particular variable are equivalent across models.[36] In general, we see results that are consistent with the figures reported here, and we also see that, despite their high intercorrelation, trust and ideology generally have independent effects on program support that varies by spending mode.

In all six program areas, those who trust the government are more supportive of social spending. And in three of the program areas (retirement savings, student loans, and green energy credits), trust has a significantly ($p < .05$) greater independent effect on program support in the direct spending frame than in the tax expenditure frame.

Ideology matters to program support in the direct spending frame for all six policy areas: when the program is framed as direct spending, liberals want government to do more. But for two of the six programs, mortgage interest and retirement savings, ideology has no impact on program support. And in five of the six areas—all but green energy subsidies—the effect of ideology is greater for direct spending programs than for tax expenditure programs. Even when the underlying subsidies are the same, in other words, direct spending programs are ideologically divisive in ways that tax expenditures are not.

Figure 4.2 Mean Levels of Social Program Support, by Spending Frame and Political Trust, 2015

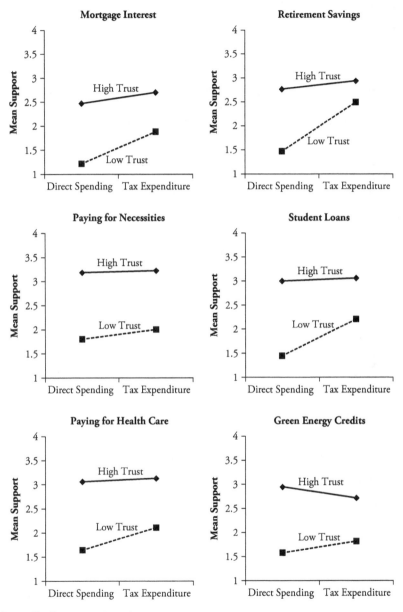

Source: YouGov survey, August 2015.

Table 4.4 Predicting Attitudes Toward Social Policy, by Spending Frame, 2015

	Mortgage Interest		Retirement Savings		Paying for Necessities	
	Direct Spending Frame	Tax Expenditure Frame	Direct Spending Frame	Tax Expenditure Frame	Direct Spending Frame	Tax Expenditure Frame
Trust in government	0.52* (0.08)	0.46* (0.08)	0.47* (0.08)	0.23* (0.08)	0.41* (0.08)	0.44* (0.08)
Ideology (liberal-conservative scale)	-0.30* (0.06)	-0.07 (0.06)	-0.27* (0.06)	0.01 (0.52)	-0.48* (0.53)	-0.32* (0.06)
Education (highest degree earned)	-0.06 (0.04)	0.02 (0.05)	0.03 (0.04)	0.05 (0.04)	-0.07 (0.04)	0.10* (0.04)
Family income	-0.05* (0.02)	0.03 (0.02)	0.03 (0.02)	0.08 (0.02)	-0.09* (0.02)	-0.02 (0.02)
Race (white)	0.03 (0.05)	-0.01 (0.05)	0.05 (0.06)	0.05 (0.04)	-0.06* (0.03)	-0.03 (0.03)
Gender (female)	0.09 (0.06)	-0.28* (0.13)	-0.14 (0.12)	-0.18 (0.05)	0.15 (0.12)	-0.01 (0.12)
Constant	2.14* (0.40)	2.17* (0.38)	2.10* (0.38)	2.36* (0.37)	2.88 (0.39)	2.71 (0.36)
N	430	430	429	431	419	445

	Student Loans		Paying for Health Care		Green Energy Credits	
	Direct Spending Frame	Tax Expenditure Frame	Direct Spending Frame	Tax Expenditure Frame	Direct Spending Frame	Tax Expenditure Frame
Trust in government	0.63* (0.08)	0.53* (0.08)	0.52* (0.08)	0.48* (0.07)	0.57* (0.07)	0.35* (0.07)
Ideology (liberal-conservative scale)	-0.33* (0.06)	-0.23* (0.06)	-0.37* (0.06)	-0.16* (0.04)	-0.31* (0.05)	-0.35* (0.05)
Education (highest degree earned)	-0.08 (0.05)	0.06 (0.04)	0.03 (0.05)	0.04 (0.04)	0.02 (0.04)	0.02 (0.04)
Family income	-0.02 (0.02)	-0.03 (0.02)	-0.02 (0.02)	-0.03 (0.02)	0.03 (0.02)	0.01 (0.02)
Race (white)	-0.02 (0.05)	0.01 (0.05)	-0.08 (0.05)	-0.12* (0.04)	0.01 (0.04)	0.04 (0.05)
Gender (female)	0.11 (0.13)	0.02 (0.12)	-0.16 (0.12)	-0.01 (0.11)	0.07 (0.10)	0.02 (0.10)
Constant	2.32* (0.43)	2.50* (0.44)	2.33* (0.38)	2.82* (0.35)	1.71* (0.33)	2.34* (0.32)
N	431	433	395	466	536	550

Source: YouGov survey, August 2015.

Note: Table entries are seemingly unrelated regression coefficients (standard errors in parentheses).

*p < .05

Trust and "Ideological Sacrifice"

The discussion in this chapter, built from the work of Thomas Rudolph and others, suggests that political trust should matter differentially for liberals and conservatives.[37] First, trust should generally matter more to the policy preferences of conservatives, given that conservatives have to "sacrifice" core ideological principles to support government spending. Second, the role of trust should be especially relevant for conservatives in the direct spending frame. While conservatives' support for tax expenditure policy still must acknowledge a government role that affects social outcomes, the fact that the money is to be spent through the tax code and the benefits are to be delivered privately helps to mitigate the "sacrifices" they must make.

Table 4.5 analyzes these issues, presenting models identical to those in table 4.4, but segmented for liberals and conservatives. (Sociodemographic controls are not shown in the tables to save space but are included in the models.) First, we see that for five of the six issues (all but mortgage interest), trust has a more direct impact on program support among conservatives than among liberals. This result is consistent with most recent work on the topic and illustrates that trust in government has a particularly important role to play in shaping support for government programs among people who might otherwise be predisposed to oppose them.

Second, we see that for three of the six issues—mortgage interest, retirement security, and green energy credits—the interaction between trust and spending frame is statistically significant, illustrating that trust matters more to program support from conservatives when the program is delivered directly than when it is delivered through the tax code. Though not consistent across all six issues, this result is consistent with our expectations, suggesting that delivering money through the tax code not only reduces aggregate levels of opposition to social policy among conservatives but also lessens the importance of trust in government in shaping that opposition. For none of the six issues is trust more important in the direct spending frame for liberals.

Figure 4.3 illustrates the substantive magnitude of these results, using the coefficients from table 4.5 to show the expected mean levels of program support for these three issues across different levels of trust. Once again, the relatively parallel slopes of the lines for liberals illustrate that trust increases support for social policy among liberals, but does so regardless

Table 4.5 Effects of Trust on Support for Social Policy, by Ideology, 2015

	Mortgage Interest		Retirement Savings		Paying for Necessities	
	Liberals	Conservatives	Liberals	Conservatives	Liberals	Conservatives
Trust in government	0.42* (0.15)	0.39* (0.16)	0.20 (0.13)	0.40* (0.15)	0.08 (0.12)	0.83* (0.15)
Direct spending frame	0.08 (0.46)	-1.53* (0.37)	-0.76* (0.40)	-1.63* (0.36)	-0.26 (0.38)	-0.14 (0.36)
Trust*direct spending frame	-0.12 (0.21)	0.45* (0.22)	0.23 (0.18)	0.35* (0.18)	0.20 (0.17)	-0.08 (0.22)
R^2	0.05	0.17	0.07	0.22	0.03	.15
N	272	307	270	307	272	309

	Student Loans		Paying for Health Care		Green Energy Credits	
	Liberals	Conservatives	Liberals	Conservatives	Liberals	Conservatives
Trust in government	0.36* (0.13)	0.84* (0.15)	0.42* (0.11)	-0.69* (0.15)	0.20* (0.11)	0.57* (0.11)
Direct spending frame	-0.29 (0.42)	-0.40 (0.37)	0.40 (0.37)	-0.80* (0.37)	0.04 (0.41)	-0.22* (0.31)
Trust*direct spending frame	0.17 (0.19)	0.12 (0.22)	-0.15 (0.17)	0.06 (0.22)	-0.01 (0.13)	0.16* (0.12)
R^2	0.05	0.18	0.06	0.16	0.01	0.14
N	273	308	271	306	317	367

Source: YouGov survey, August 2015.

Note: Table entries are seemingly unrelated regression coefficients (standard errors in parentheses).

$*p < .05$

Figure 4.3 Expected Social Program Support from Liberals and Conservatives, by Level of Trust, 2015

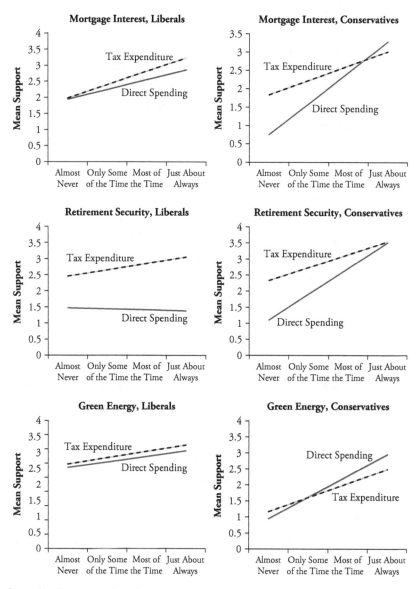

Source: YouGov survey, August 2015.

of how benefits are delivered. For conservatives, the results are different. Expected program support for the (relatively few) conservatives who trust the government differ little, if at all, across spending mode: for this group, high levels of trust are expected to essentially negate the role of ideology. But for conservatives who distrust the government, delivery mode becomes even more important: support for direct spending programs among distrustful conservatives is very close to zero, while tax expenditure programs, though generally not as popular as they are among liberals, are expected to be at least somewhat well supported by conservatives.

Ideology and Trust in the "Real World"

Finally, after exploring the relative impact of ideology and trust in the experimental setting, we look at the role that each plays in shaping support for or opposition to actual social programs. Our module of the 2014 CCES asked respondents for their views on a subset of the tax expenditure programs discussed in chapter 3: those designed to subsidize low-income work, to provide tax credits to parents paying tuition for their dependent children, to encourage tax-free 401(k) contributions, and to enable the purchase of health insurance with pretax income.

Though we again highly stylized the descriptions of these programs when portraying them to respondents (the wording for these questions was identical to the wording replicated in chapter 3), our intent was to portray tax breaks as they exist in current federal policy. This survey also asked respondents about their views on spending (using the standard GSS wording described earlier) in four areas in which the government currently spends money: assistance to the poor, efforts to keep college affordable, Social Security, and public health. Our questions thus addressed attitudes in four programmatic areas (helping the less well-off, paying for college, promoting retirement security, and paying for health care). The disadvantage compared to our experimental setup, of course, was that these programs are not identical to one another across spending mode in either target or intent. The advantage was that we could describe these programs straightforwardly as actual programs in which the government currently invested.

For each program, we estimate seemingly unrelated regression models predicting program support (on a 0–4 scale, ranging from "strongly oppose" to "strongly support") for liberal and conservative respondents as a function

Table 4.6 Predicting Social Program Support as a Function of Trust, by Ideology, 2015

	β_{trust}(Liberals)	β_{trust}(Conservatives)	Probability That Coefficients Are Equal to One Another
Tax expenditures			
Subsidizing low-income work	0.10* (0.05)	0.16* (0.06)	0.41
Tuition credits for parents	0.04* (0.06)	0.10* (0.05)	0.58
Contributing to retirement plans	0.03 (0.05)	0.03 (0.05)	0.91
Purchasing health insurance	0.03 (0.04)	0.05 (0.04)	0.79
Direct spending			
Welfare spending	0.11 (0.05)	0.27* (0.05)	0.05
Helping the poor	0.18* (0.05)	0.27* (0.05)	0.18
Keeping college affordable	0.06 (0.04)	0.25* (0.06)	<0.01
Social Security	−0.04 (0.04)	0.13* (0.05)	<0.01
Public health	0.02 (0.04)	0.27* (0.06)	<0.01

Source: YouGov survey, August 2015.

Note: Table entries are seemingly unrelated regression coefficients (standard errors in parentheses).

*$p < .05$

of trust and each of the demographic correlates used in our experimental results. Table 4.6 presents a streamlined version of the results. The first two columns show the coefficient for trust on program support for each of the programs for liberals and conservatives. The third column presents a χ^2 test of parameter equivalence for this coefficient across the liberal and conservative models.

For the tax expenditure programs, we find that while trust occasionally matters to program support, it does not do so differentially for liberals and conservatives. This makes sense given our expectations: for conservatives, support for tax expenditures requires less ideological sacrifice than support for direct spending programs, so it is no surprise that trust in government does not matter more for conservatives than it does for liberals.

When it comes to direct spending, however, we see that the coefficient for trust in the models for conservative respondents is substantially higher than in the models for liberal respondents, and that, for three of the four issue sets, trust is a significantly greater predictor of support for conservatives than it is for liberals. This again reinforces our expectation that supporting direct spending programs is "harder" for conservatives than supporting tax expenditure programs, and that a higher level of trust in government is required in order to feel confident in supporting them.[38] Of note is that these direct spending questions, like the GSS questions but unlike our experimental questions, did not prime the idea of "government" explicitly, but rather simply asked whether "we" are spending too much or too little to address them. If we had reminded respondents that "government" is actually doing the spending, the effects of trust on support from conservatives would probably have been even larger.

Conclusion

This chapter has used a series of experimental vignettes to explore the impact of program delivery mechanism on support for social policy. Though the results are not perfectly consistent across models, this analysis reveals several things. First and most importantly, we find that social policy is more popular when benefits are delivered through the tax code than when benefits are delivered directly by government. This is true regardless of the popularity of the underlying social goal and regardless of the policy's likely consequences. The impact of program delivery mechanism on popularity is especially powerful for those whose opposition to government intervention in the economy is either ideological (political conservatives) or pragmatic (those who distrust government), strongly suggesting that tax expenditures are more popular because they do not prime the idea of "government" as explicitly as direct spending does.

Consistent with what we saw in chapter 3, citizens form preferences on tax expenditure policies in ways that, at least at the margins, are different from the ways in which they form opinions on direct spending. In particular, the common heuristics that drive opinions on social spending policy, like ideology, do not apply—or at least do not apply as strongly—to opinions on social tax policy. This chapter has shown that this is the case even when the underlying goals and cost of a particular social policy are the same.

The implications for both the design and framing of social policy programs are considerable. The public is ambivalent about the role of government in solving problems—on the one hand, Americans have an egalitarian impulse and support intervention to provide opportunity and reduce inequality. But on the other hand, people dislike "big government" in the abstract and have little faith in government's ability to do things well. The essential contradiction is this: Americans want a stronger social welfare state, but they also want a smaller, leaner government. The relatively good fit of tax expenditures with both roles—small government, and a strong system of social welfare—suggests that such programs have a "framing advantage" that makes it easier for policymakers to persuade the public to support private rather than public solutions for social problems. Tax expenditure programs, in other words, make it possible for policymakers to claim that a program finances popular social goals while also allowing them to largely avoid the specter of "government involvement." Direct social spending, by contrast, fulfills public demands for more social services, but conflicts with public impulses to limit government.

In short, at the margins, those in favor of privatizing social services through tax expenditure policy should have an easier time mobilizing public support for their plans, particularly by pitting these programs against similar programs financed through direct means. If citizens perceive benefits as being delivered by the private sector, or see that people are able to reduce their tax bill by engaging in particular behaviors, then expansion of social policy in a given area is more likely to be seen as providing people with incentives to help themselves than as setting up another "big government program."

Another implication of these results is that those who wish to protect existing tax expenditure programs, even highly regressive ones, are advantaged by the fact that these programs are viewed in a more positive light than they would be if the same benefits were delivered through direct payments. It is difficult to imagine the mortgage interest tax deduction being as popular as it is, for example, if the government simply sent recipients checks in an amount largely based on the value of the recipient's home. Our experimental results suggested as much. But because this deduction is "hidden" in the tax code, the actual cost and impact of the social tax program are shielded from public view.[39] The fact that even progressive presidents have added to or resisted challenging entrenched tax expenditure programs speaks to the high level of support for such programs.

The moderating role of ideology and trust also tells us something important about the construction of social welfare policy. The fact that the effects of the delivery mechanism frame were stronger for conservatives than liberals could explain why Republicans, even though generally opposed to the idea of "big government," also on balance broadly agree that inequality is a problem that requires a collective solution and that the government has a role to play in providing opportunity and improving social outcomes.[40] At least some conservatives might view tax expenditure policy as a way to have its policy cake and eat it too: it allows them to provide desirable social benefits while still adhering to the values of individual initiative and supporting the private sector.

In an era of low and declining trust in government, those seeking to expand or protect social policy in particular areas face an uphill battle in convincing Americans—even those sympathetic to the overall goals of a policy—that government can be expected to do its job well. Spending money through the tax code might convey particular advantages in this environment as well. When citizens trust the government to do what is right, then delivering a program through the tax code offers no particular advantage: what matters is whether government is helping the people it is supposed to help. But when citizens are skeptical of government, then delivering benefits through the tax code overcomes some of the hurdles associated with expanding social policy to a public increasingly unconvinced that government will work the way it is supposed to.

So far we have learned that tax expenditure programs are popular, at least in part, because they minimize the negative associations with "big government" that lead many people to oppose social policy. They also tend to scramble, or at least minimize, standard ideological divisions over the size and scope of government. Of course, we know that support for or opposition to social spending in particular domains is not simply a function of ideological or efficiency-based arguments, but is also grounded more simply in views of *who* is benefiting from government assistance: in other words, are the people receiving aid deserving of what they are getting? In the next chapter, we turn to views of social policy beneficiaries themselves, seeking to understand how the mode of social spending affects not only support for policies but also the views of those benefiting from them.

CHAPTER 5

Deservingness, Race, and Social Spending

THE TWO LARGEST means-tested poverty assistance programs in the United States are Temporary Assistance for Needy Families (TANF) and the Earned Income Tax Credit (EITC). In 1996, the federal government replaced Aid to Families with Dependent Children (AFDC) with TANF in an effort to reform a program that many detractors saw as discouraging marriage, deemphasizing the importance of work, and encouraging dependency on government aid. Both President Clinton and the Republican Congress promoted TANF as a reform that would provide government assistance to the poor in a way that incentivized work and supported traditional family structures.[1]

The Earned Income Tax Credit shares many of the same broad policy goals as TANF, and like TANF, it was passed with bipartisan support. Enacted during the Ford administration as part of the Tax Reduction Act of 1975, the EITC is a refundable tax credit that essentially subsidizes low-wage work: refundable tax credits are targeted at low-income workers (phasing out at higher income levels), and the largest benefits are provided to the neediest recipients.[2]

Though TANF is more generous to families with children and does not tie benefits as directly to paid work as does the EITC, the racial and demographic compositions of beneficiaries of these two programs are quite comparable.[3] The programs also share the same policy goals of encouraging employment, stabilizing traditional families, and reducing the role of the federal government in providing aid to the poor. In spite of their similar goals, however, the EITC and TANF have developed at much different rates over the last four decades. The EITC has expanded its eligibility requirements to adjust for family size and include single adults without children, and it was indexed to inflation as part of the Tax Reform Act of 1986. In addition, the actual value of the benefit was increased in 1990, 1993, 2001, and 2009. There have been only incremental changes in TANF funding over this same period, however, and since 2010, Congress has extended TANF with short-term bills in lieu of a full reauthorization of the program.

Owing to these differential changes, the EITC overtook TANF/AFDC as the federal government's primary way of providing cash assistance to low-income families in 1993. The federal government now spends three times as much money on the EITC as it does on "conventional" welfare programs. How policymakers debate the future of these programs also differs substantially: an expansion (or retrenchment) of traditional welfare programs remains the subject of bitter partisan fights, while even prominent Republican policymakers have entertained the idea of expanding the EITC.

These changes have been driven, or at least are reflected, by public taste and demand for the programs. Welfare stands nearly alone in its unpopularity among domestic spending programs. The General Social Survey has asked about preferences for welfare spending in every iteration of the survey since 1973: even without reminding people that welfare money comes from tax dollars or using any of the other phrases that typically dampen support for social spending programs among the public, pluralities of survey respondents have said that the United States spends "too much" on welfare in every year that the question has been asked. The Earned Income Tax Credit, by contrast, typically enjoys majority support.

What makes traditional welfare spending so unpopular while the EITC remains popular? Much research in political science and elsewhere tells us that this difference is attributable in large part to how citizens view the deservingness of their beneficiaries: welfare recipients are stereotyped as lazy and unwilling to help themselves, while recipients of the EITC are seen as working hard to get ahead. In this chapter, we examine the issue of "deservingness" in social spending more broadly. Arguing that the means through which social benefits are delivered conditions how citizens think about both the worth of social programs and the deservingness of their beneficiaries, we pay particular attention to the critical role of the delivery mode in shaping perceptions of deservingness.

Through an analysis of several types of social spending programs, both real and hypothetical, we find that programs that deliver benefits through the tax code prime different considerations than programs that deliver benefits directly, and that these different considerations lead people to view both the worth of the programs and the deservingness of their beneficiaries in different ways. Delivering programs through the tax code, in other words, affects how Americans think not only about government spending but about the people who benefit from it.

The Deservingness Heuristic

As noted in earlier chapters, a number of factors influence citizens' support for or opposition to social welfare policies, including partisanship, trust in government, self-interest, and values, to name just a few.[4] But perhaps most prominent in the social-psychological literature on this subject is a simple consideration of whether particular beneficiaries of social assistance are deserving of the aid they receive.[5]

This "deservingness heuristic" undergirds much of how citizens make sense of social policy: above and beyond cultural or partisan predispositions, citizens wish to bestow government aid on those they perceive as unlucky or working to better themselves, and they would rather withhold benefits from those whom they view as lazy or unsympathetic. Simple perceptions of the deservingness of aid recipients very often supersede more politically salient value orientations in shaping support for government spending—broader political orientations such as egalitarianism and support for markets are less important to attitudes toward social spending when citizens are asked to focus on their views of aid recipients themselves. Some policymakers know this: seeking to win support for government spending cuts and welfare state retrenchment, they often focus their messaging on the possibility that beneficiaries of spending do not deserve it.[6]

The power of the deservingness heuristic reflects, at least in part, a desire among humans to reward people who are likely to cooperate and do "their fair share" in bettering society and to punish those who might seek to cheat the system or "free-ride" off the work of others.[7] The ability to both identify and reward "reciprocators" while punishing "cheaters" was central to the survival of early human societies of all types.[8] It remains a fairly universal trait across nearly all types of societies and cultures.[9]

This explains why the deservingness heuristic is a universal feature of public attitudes toward social welfare spending: perceptions of deservingness are strongly associated with attitudes toward social welfare programs even in countries with more pro-government or communalistic orientations.[10] But this heuristic is particularly strong in the United States, especially with respect to the sharp lines many Americans draw between the so-called deserving and undeserving poor.[11] The general tendency to offer relatively limited and conditional benefits to the poor signals a particular conception of deservingness in the United States that, at least to some extent, blames lower-income citizens for their plight.[12]

In practical terms, what does a "deserving" beneficiary look like? Van Oorschot identified several characteristics of beneficiaries that shape whether they are likely to be considered deserving or not.[13] These include objective criteria, such as degree of need, as well as more subjective perceptions of beneficiaries—whether they are grateful for the aid they receive, for instance, or whether they have contributed to society or are expected to meaningfully do so. For Americans, deservingness means playing by the rules and looking to better one's own circumstances in life without seeking (or having) unfair advantages. Deserving beneficiaries are those who are suffering hardship through no fault of their own, or who wish to use government aid as a "bridge" to a future when they will no longer need such aid. And perhaps most of all, deserving beneficiaries are those who are hard workers. Broader American value orientations—perhaps rooted in historically individualistic or even Calvinistic conceptions of human nature— have as a central tenet a belief in both the importance and value of hard work as a means to get ahead.[14] In the United States, individual agency is viewed as central to the ability to get ahead, and Americans, more than citizens of almost any other Western democracy, believe that differences in effort rather than circumstances beyond one's control are responsible for differences in economic outcomes.[15]

One reason Americans dislike welfare, then, is that they believe that welfare recipients are simply lazy.[16] Recent data bear this out: the top half of table 5.1 shows results from our August 2015 survey asking respondents how well certain terms describe people currently receiving welfare bene-

Table 5.1 Americans' Perceptions of Welfare and Social Security Recipients, 2016

"How well do the following words describe people who are receiving welfare benefits?"

	Lazy	Hardworking	Industrious	Unmotivated
Very well	19%	11%	8%	24%
Somewhat well	32	33	28	30
Not very well	29	34	37	29
Not well at all	19	21	26	16

"How well do the following words describe people who are receiving Social Security benefits?"

	Lazy	Hardworking	Industrious	Unmotivated
Very well	6%	30%	25%	6%
Somewhat well	11	38	37	15
Not very well	28	19	23	32
Not well at all	53	11	12	45

Source: YouGov survey, August 2016.

fits. More than half of respondents said that the words "lazy" and "unmotivated" describe welfare recipients at least somewhat well; a significantly lower percentage said that the terms "hardworking" and "industrious" described welfare recipients at least somewhat well. This result may reflect the view that welfare recipients are not working.

But contrast this view of welfare recipients to how Americans describe recipients of the very popular Social Security program (bottom half of table 5.1): even though Social Security benefits are by definition given to people above retirement age, and despite Social Security having strict requirements against working more than a certain number of hours to receive full benefits, a significant majority of Americans describe recipients of Social Security benefits as hardworking and precious few say that they are lazy.

Explaining Perceptions of Deservingness

Though the basic importance of deservingness is common across people and cultures, including the general types of traits associated with deservingness, there are both individual and contextual differences in who is seen as deserving. At the individual level, certain kinds of people have broader or different conceptions of what it means to be deserving than others.

Some of these differences are rooted in broader political values. The belief systems of conservatives and individualists, for example, make them skeptical of government intervention, and thus, in order to justify their opposition to spending to help the needy, they are more apt to see individuals in need as being in that position because of their personal failings.[17] Liberals and egalitarians, on the other hand, are more apt to see people in need as the victims of circumstances outside of their control.[18] Self-interest also plays a role, as people are more apt to see those who look like them, or those with similar life circumstances, as more deserving than others.[19]

Contextually, however, views on who should be seen as deserving and who should not is in part socially constructed. The social construction of a target group—defined by Anne Schneider and Helen Ingram as the "cultural characterizations or popular images whose behavior and well-being are affected by public policy"—influences how certain social or economic groups are perceived.[20] Schneider and Ingram's classic typology of the social constructions of particular target groups is strongly rooted in the idea of deservingness.[21] Positively viewed groups are seen as playing by the rules and as being either in need of help through no fault of their own (because they have children, are elderly, or are working single parents) or as belonging to groups with resources that are deployed to the betterment of society (small businesses, investors, the middle class). Negatively viewed groups are seen as either "cheating" the system or as holding views or engaging in behaviors perceived as threatening to those who do play by the rules (criminals, the unemployed not seeking work, large banks).

Figure 5.1 illustrates this point. Respondents in our August 2015 survey were presented with a list of different social groups and asked simply to rate how deserving each group was of government aid. With few exceptions, the figure shows that the groups seen as most deserving of aid were those who are positively constructed in the Schneider and Ingram terminology, while those seen as least deserving were those who are negatively constructed.

A particular group's social construction, in turn, is strongly connected to the types of options that might be realistically available to assist them: both policymakers and citizens will be more willing to invest resources to assist groups viewed positively rather than negatively.[22] How particular targets of government aid are viewed, in other words, conditions the types of policy benefits that can be feasibly delivered to them.[23]

Figure 5.1 Americans' Perceptions of the Deservingness of Various Social Groups, 2016

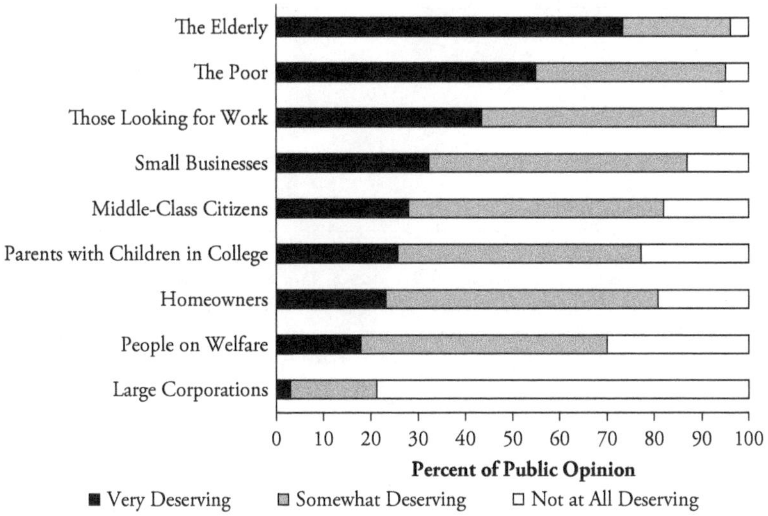

Source: YouGov survey, August 2016.
Note: Respondents were asked: "Below is a list of groups and institutions that are often talked about as targets for government assistance. For each, please tell me whether you believe this group is very deserving, only somewhat deserving, or not at all deserving of financial assistance from the federal government."

Race and the Construction of Deservingness

The role of race and racial prejudice in the United States deserves special consideration for its role in shaping perceptions of deservingness and, in turn, policy. Many white citizens believe that African Americans are less committed to the American value of a strong work ethic.[24] Paul Sniderman and Thomas Piazza argue that whites' opposition to programs that help African Americans is driven largely by how they view this group's effort—that is, their perception that black citizens as a group lack a work ethic and therefore are undeserving of government aid.[25]

Table 5.2, using data from a module of our August 2016 survey, illustrates race-based differences in perceptions of work ethic: this question simply borrows from a standard American National Election Study scale asking respondents to rate both white and black Americans on a seven-point scale from "lazy" to "hardworking." The table presents data for the responses of white respondents: on average, white respondents rated the work ethic of

Table 5.2 Americans' Perceptions of the Work Ethic of Whites and Blacks, 2016

	Whites	Blacks
1 (lazy)	2%	5%
2	2	7
3	6	12
4	27	32
5	17	16
6	20	10
7 (hardworking)	27	18

Source: YouGov survey, August 2016.

Note: Respondents were asked: "imagine a seven-point scale on which the characteristics of the people in a group can be rated. In the first question a score of 1 means that you think almost all of the people in that group tend to be 'hardworking.' A score of 7 means that you think most people in the group are 'lazy.' A score of 4 means that you think that most people in the group are not closer to one end or the other, and of course, you may choose any number in between. Where would you place [group] on this scale?"

whites more than 10 percent higher than that of blacks. Sixty-three percent of white respondents placed the work ethic of whites above the midpoint on the scale; only 44 percent rated the work ethic of blacks above the midpoint. The perceived undeservingness of African Americans, rooted in a perceived lack of work ethic, explains at least in part the resistance of white Americans to programs designed to benefit racial minorities. For some, programs designed explicitly to help African Americans attempt to help those who do not deserve aid.

These attitudes spill over even into opinions on programs that are ostensibly race-neutral, since Americans tend to overestimate the proportion of nonwhite beneficiaries of these programs.[26] In perhaps the most definitive treatment of the topic, Martin Gilens argues that "it is now widely believed that welfare is a 'race-coded' topic that evokes racial imagery and attitudes, even when racial minorities are not explicitly mentioned."[27] The widespread belief that African Americans lack a commitment to a work ethic plays an important part in structuring white attitudes toward welfare spending: broadly speaking, this research has shown that antipoverty programs are less popular than they otherwise would be both because they activate racial prejudices explicitly and because they drive perceptions of whether the beneficiaries of such programs are deserving, as conditioned by racial prejudices.

Nevertheless, not all antipoverty programs are subject to the same types of negative stereotyping of their beneficiaries—not even those thought by the public to benefit mostly racial and ethnic minorities. Compared to programs such as welfare, Gilens writes, "programs that are seen as enhancing the ability of the poor to support themselves, rather than rewarding the lazy with government handouts, do not evoke the same negative imagery."[28] White Americans are not necessarily opposed to social programs that disproportionately help racial minorities, as long as the programs are perceived as benefiting "deserving" minorities.

The Impact of Social Spending Mode on Perceptions of Deservingness

The social construction of particular beneficiaries or hypothetical beneficiaries of government aid comes from many sources: the media, the actions of strategic politicians, and deep-seated notions of what it means to be "deserving" of help. We argue, however, that the delivery mechanism for benefits also matters for how citizens see their beneficiaries. In other words, while perceptions of beneficiaries of social programs can condition the range of policy tools available to assist them, the causal arrow also goes in the other direction: the means through which policy benefits are delivered, we argue, also conditions perceptions about beneficiaries.

When citizens are faced with thinking about whether the beneficiaries of a particular social benefit are deserving of aid, a wide variety of different considerations may come into play: personal ideology and values, personal experiences with the program or its recipients, positive or negative stereotypes about beneficiaries, an evaluation of whether the program is likely to encourage positive behavior (for example, working) or negative behavior (being lazy), and views of the social goals promoted by the program itself.[29]

For many people, these considerations are in tension with one another: someone may abstractly support the goal of reducing poverty in the United States, for example, while at the same time thinking that poor citizens who receive government aid are lazy and unsympathetic.[30] Classic theories of public opinion formation tell us that the types of considerations most prominent in the minds of citizens when they are thinking about these issues matter most to the opinions they ultimately express on them.[31]

We argue that social benefits delivered through the tax code lead citizens evaluating a program's worth and the deservingness of its beneficiaries to think about different factors than they would when thinking about benefits delivered through direct spending. There are a number of reasons why we hold these expectations. First, programs delivered through the tax code prime the notion of "taxpayer" rather than "government beneficiary."[32] While Americans have complex views on the role of taxes in facilitating social spending, taxpayers are generally viewed in a positive light as people playing by the rules and doing what is necessary to help society function.[33] Williamson's work on this topic shows that Americans are proud to be considered taxpayers, because taxpayers are those who are fulfilling their basic civic responsibilities in the effort to better society.[34]

People receiving money through the tax code, in other words, are viewed as more deserving at least in part because they are seen as simply getting back some of what they have already paid into the system. In this way, delivering benefits through the tax code may help to construct the target group as being more sympathetic than delivering benefits through other means. This might be especially true when delivering benefits to groups who are perceived as unsympathetic and not deserving of aid—either those who are not working and thus are viewed as not trying to better themselves, or those who are wealthy and often viewed with resentment.[35]

Programs delivered through direct government payments, by contrast, prime several negative connotations. The first of these is the notion of "government spending." As we discussed in chapter 4, on least at the abstract, symbolic level, "government" is viewed as wasteful and inefficient.[36] While Americans may like many particular types of social spending (particularly on groups that are perceived to be in need through no fault of their own), attitudes toward government spending more abstractly defined are generally more negative.[37] And as Gilens and others have noted, the notion of "receiving checks" from the government can also prime strong racial connotations: recipients of government spending are both portrayed in the media and perceived by citizens as disproportionately black and disproportionately undeserving.[38]

In addition, the program design of social tax expenditures comports well with the public's long-standing ambivalence about social welfare spending— that is, the tendency among many citizens to favor a more equal society in which government does more to solve social problems and the commonly held view that government intervention is suspect and government's ability to solve social problems efficiently or effectively cannot be trusted.[39] These competing attitudes lead to a tension in attitudes toward many types of direct spending: people want government to solve important social problems, but they also prefer a smaller and less directly intrusive government.[40] Social tax expenditures, by incentivizing the private provision of social benefits, reduce this tension by aligning with both views, reconciling distrust of government with a desire to solve social problems: they are seen to incentivize individual initiative and private effort, while also working to achieve particular popular social outcomes.[41]

Social benefits delivered through the tax code, then, negate two negative signals commonly associated with direct spending designed to assist the poor: the negative and often racially charged view of "recipients of government aid," and the view of government as inefficient and not to be trusted, more broadly defined. We believe that these differences in program delivery mechanism should affect how respondents perceive the beneficiaries of government aid. More directly, we expect that people portrayed as receiving aid through the tax code will be seen as more deserving of what they receive than people who receive aid directly. Given that aid given through the tax code should be less likely to prime racialized considerations in the minds of citizens, we also expect that recipients of tax expenditure programs will be viewed through a less racialized lens than recipients of direct spending programs.

Spending Mode and Deservingness

To explore the role of spending mode in shaping perceptions of government beneficiaries, we turn to experiments similar to those employed in chapter 4: taking otherwise identical frames of a particular social benefit and varying the means through which it is delivered. Instead of looking at views of the programs themselves, however, we look at views of the recipients of such benefits, in particular views of how deserving they are of the aid they receive. We build from the work of Lene Aarøe and Michael Petersen, who use a vignette-based approach to understanding how citizens view the deservingness of recipients of government assistance.[42]

We asked respondents in nationally representative surveys taken in January and August 2016 to think about six different hypothetical recipients of government aid in the following vignettes. Three recipients receive downwardly distributing aid: a man receives aid to pay for basic necessities in lieu of having a regular job (referred to here as the "paying for necessities" vignette); a married couple receive aid to purchase publicly subsidized health insurance for their low-income family ("public health care"); and a man receives aid to subsidize his earnings from a low-wage job ("wage subsidies"). Three of the beneficiaries receive upwardly distributing aid: subsidies for their contributions to an employer-matched retirement program ("contributing to retirement"); subsidies to purchase health care through an employer-based plan ("private health care"); and subsidies that offset their interest payments on a mortgage ("mortgage interest"). In all six vignettes, we add either specific markers of the income of the recipient ("think of a family of four earning roughly $200,000 per year") or other economic indicators that the recipient is either well-off or facing hardship ("think of a young man who has been out of work for some time") relative to the general population.

As in chapter 4, in each of these six vignettes we varied information about how government benefits would be provided to citizens: some would receive direct payments from the government, and some would receive benefits through the tax code. Again, the goal was to hold constant all information about the aid received, save for the means through which the benefits would be delivered. Wording for these vignettes is as follows:

Paying for Necessities

Direct spending: "Think of a young man who has been out of work for some time. He has a high school degree and once had a regular job, but has not been able to find work that suits his expectations. The man receives federal assistance in the form of monthly checks that help him pay for groceries and basic necessities."

Tax expenditure: "Think of a young man who has been out of work for some time. He has a high school degree and once had a regular job, but has not been able to find work that suits his expectations. The man receives federal assistance in the form of a federal tax refund that helps him pay for groceries and basic necessities."

Public Health Care

Direct spending: "Think of a lower-middle-class family of four. Neither parent works at a job that provides health insurance benefits. The family receives federal assistance in the form of a health insurance plan that is paid for in part using subsidies from the federal government."

Tax expenditure: "Think of a lower-middle-class family of four. Neither parent works at a job that provides health insurance benefits. The family receives federal assistance in the form of a tax break that allows them to deduct their health insurance premium from their taxable income."

Wage Subsidies

Direct spending: "Think of a working father of two. He earns $18,000 a year working at a large retail chain. He also benefits from a federal program designed to supplement his income by providing him with a refund on his federal tax bill. He receives about $3,000 in federal tax credits per year."

Tax expenditure: "Think of a working father of two. He earns $18,000 a year working at a large retail chain. He also benefits from a federal program that sends him money designed to supplement his income. He receives about $3,000 in payments per year from the federal government."

Contributing to Retirement

Direct spending: "Think of a man earning roughly $100,000 per year. He works at a full-time job and his contributions to a retirement plan are matched by his employer. He benefits from a government program that sends him annual payments to help offset the amount that he contributes to his retirement plan."

Tax expenditure: "Think of a man earning roughly $100,000 per year. He works at a full-time job and his contributions to a retirement plan are matched by his employer. He benefits from a government program that allows him to exclude his retirement contributions from his taxable income, thus reducing the amount of money he pays in federal taxes."

Private Health Care

Direct spending: "Think of a family of four earning roughly $200,000 per year. Both parents work at full-time jobs and receive health insurance coverage that is paid for in part by their employers. The family benefits from a federal program that sends them annual checks to help offset their own contributions to their health coverage."

Tax expenditure: "Think of a family of four earning roughly $200,000 per year. Both parents work at full-time jobs and receive health insurance coverage that is paid for in part by their employers. The family benefits from a federal program that allows them to exclude their own contributions to their health coverage from their taxable income, thus reducing the amount of money they pay in federal taxes."

Mortgage Interest

Direct spending: "Think of a family of four earning roughly $150,000 per year. Both parents work at full-time jobs, and the family lives in a five-bedroom home in a suburban neighborhood. The family benefits from a federal program that sends them monthly checks from the government to offset the amount they pay in interest on their home mortgage."

Tax expenditure: "Think of a family of four earning roughly $150,000 per year. Both parents work at full-time jobs, and the family lives in a five-bedroom home in a suburban neighborhood. The family benefits from a federal program that allows them to deduct the amount they pay in interest on their home mortgage from their federal income tax bill."

For each question, respondents were asked how deserving (very, somewhat, not very, or not at all) recipients are of the aid they receive. Respondents were randomly selected into one of these two "delivery frames" separately for each of the three programs.[43]

Who Is Deserving?

Figure 5.2 shows the mean perceived level of deservingness (on the 1–4 scale just described) for each of the six hypothetical recipients. This figure collapses across spending mode conditions. The figure shows that, overall, perceptions of deservingness varied across recipients in ways that comport with what we know about the deservingness heuristic more generally. Sympathetic beneficiaries (those facing hardship who are also portrayed as working to help themselves) were perceived as the most deserving of aid, while those who are less sympathetic (either wealthy or seemingly unwilling to work) were perceived as less deserving.

Figure 5.2 Mean Perceived Deservingness of Aid Beneficiaries, 2016

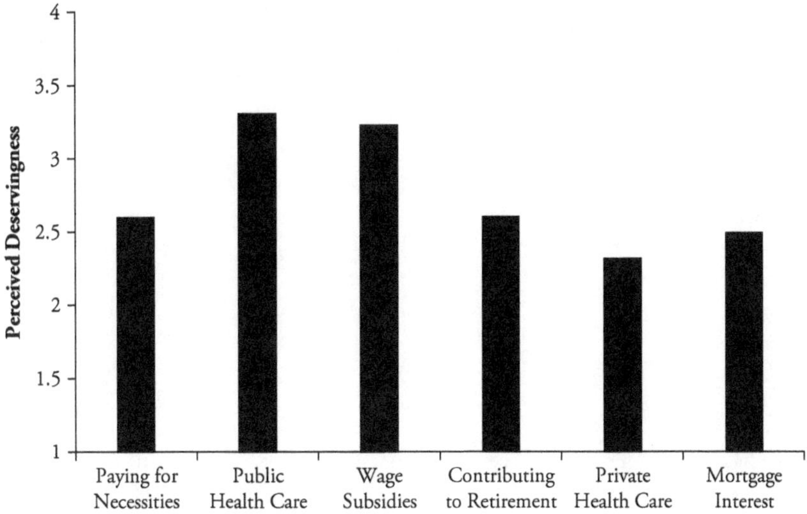

Source: YouGov survey, August 2016.

Table 5.3 shows results of a simple ordinary least squares (OLS) regression analysis that predicts deservingness (again, collapsing across spending mode condition) as a function of individual-level covariates. Results here also reinforce what we learned from chapter 4, as well as what we know about variations in perceptions of deservingness across individuals. In the three downwardly distributing vignettes, ideological self-identification and egalitarianism predict perceptions of deservingness, with conservatives less likely to view these recipients as worthy of government aid.[44] This comports with, among other things, John Jost's system justification theory, which suggests that conservatives have psychological incentives to view people facing hardship as not being worthy of assistance.[45]

We see that trust in government also makes a difference across all six vignettes; perhaps not surprisingly, given the results in chapter 4, perceptions of the beneficiaries of government assistance are inextricable from perceptions of the government providing that assistance. And though the results are more inconsistent, women and nonwhites tend to view government aid recipients as more deserving, consistent with the view that historically marginalized groups tend to view beneficiaries of government assistance more sympathetically.

Table 5.3 Predicting Perceptions of the Deservingness of Aid Recipients, 2016

	Paying for Necessities	Public Health Care	Wage Subsidies	Contributing to Retirement	Private Health Care	Mortgage Interest
Ideology (liberal-conservative scale)	−.09*	−.12*	−.07*	.02	.03	−.03
Education (highest degree earned)	−.06*	.00	−.00	.04	.03	.03
Family income	.00	−.00	−.00	.00	.00	.00
Trust in government	.21*	.14*	.11*	.21*	.23*	.17*
Egalitarianism	.12*	.13*	.13*	−.01	−.01	−.02
Race (white)	−.12*	−.12*	.09	−.10	−.14*	−.22*
Gender (female)	.06	.11*	.22*	.04	−.00	.06
R^2	.23	.29	.25	.06	.08	.08
N	1,048	1,050	1,048	1,075	1,074	1,074

Source: YouGov survey, August 2016.

Note: Estimates are OLS regression coefficients.

*$p < .05$

Who Is Perceived as Deserving?

What we see above provides confidence that the vignettes we have created produce results consistent with what is known about the deservingness heuristic: people belonging to groups that are viewed positively are seen as more deserving than those belonging to groups that are not seen as deserving, and perceptions of deservingness vary across individual respondents in predictable ways. But above and beyond these well-known characteristics, we see clear evidence that the mode in which respondents receive aid conditions how respondents perceive them.

Table 5.4 illustrates these effects, showing frequency distributions and mean levels of deservingness for each of the six vignettes, broken down by spending mode treatment. In five of the six vignettes, those who receive aid through the tax code were viewed as more deserving than those who

Table 5.4 Perceived Deservingness of Government Aid Recipients, by Spending Mode, 2016

	Paying for Necessities		Public Health Care		Wage Subsidies	
	Direct Spending	Tax Expenditure	Direct Spending	Tax Expenditure	Direct Spending	Tax Expenditure
Very deserving	17%	22%	46%	51%	52%	44%
Somewhat deserving	35	35	37	37	31	38
Not very deserving	35	31	10	9	11	12
Not at all deserving	14	13	6	2	6	7
Mean deservingness	2.54	2.66*	3.24	3.38*	3.29	3.17
N	386	409	392	431	395	384

	Contributing to Retirement		Private Health Care		Mortgage Interest	
	Direct Spending	Tax Expenditure	Direct Spending	Tax Expenditure	Direct Spending	Tax Expenditure
Very deserving	10%	30%	20%	33%	13%	30%
Somewhat deserving	21	30	26	34	19	36
Not very deserving	33	25	32	22	36	23
Not at all deserving	35	16	22	11	32	11
Mean deservingness	2.27	2.94*	2.10	2.56*	2.15	2.85*
N	591	605	603	593	593	603

Source: YouGov survey, August 2016.

*p < .05

receive identical aid through direct means. The results are strongest for the upwardly distributing programs. For example, two-thirds of respondents rated those receiving mortgage interest subsidies through the tax code as at least "somewhat deserving" of aid. When that same aid was portrayed as being received through direct means, fewer than one-third of respondents rated recipients as at least "somewhat deserving." Similar results obtain for the private health care and retirement subsidy vignettes. In all three cases, the impact of spending mode treatment dwarfs the impact of any other individual-level predictor of deservingness.

These results are supportive of our theory. Though these vignettes do not prime any deeply negative perceptions of aid recipients (that they obtained their wealth through unethical means, for example), they are designed to showcase recipients who otherwise might not be viewed sympathetically, or who may even be viewed with resentment. These recipients are generally quite well-off and doing things, like owning an expensive home, that are out of the reach of many Americans. In short, respondents may not be apt to think of them as deserving government assistance. But saying that they receive this aid through the tax code also highlights their status as taxpayers and explains that money they have already earned and paid into the system is being returned to them. Tax code spending, in other words, highlights considerations in the minds of respondents that make them more likely to view beneficiaries sympathetically.

Though less stark, similar results obtain for the downwardly distributing programs: in two of the three cases, recipients were viewed as more deserving when they received aid through the tax code. Again, the results for experimental treatment are on par with other important individual-level predictors of perceptions of deservingness. In the "paying for necessities" vignette, for example, the difference in mean deservingness perceptions across spending mode treatment is more than half the size of the difference in mean deservingness perceptions between ideological liberals and conservatives, despite deep ideological divides in how to view beneficiaries of public assistance programs of this sort.[46]

So far we have seen that spending mode matters not just to how we see government programs but also to how we see those who benefit from them. Tax code–based spending seems to lead respondents to view beneficiaries through the more positively valenced lens of "taxpayer" rather than the more negatively valenced lens of "aid recipient," especially when beneficiaries have other qualities that might lead them to be viewed as undeserving recipients. In what follows, we build on these analyses, in particular exploring the role that spending mode might play in either enhancing or dampening the impact of support for spending programs generally and, more specifically, how it affects perceptions of their beneficiaries.

Race and Social Spending Support

As much as or more than any other factor, racial prejudices drive preferences for social spending programs in the United States.[47] Programs perceived, rightly or wrongly, as benefiting those who are not working to better themselves are generally unpopular, and perceptions of the work ethic of program beneficiaries are often strongly connected to deep-seated racial stereotypes and prejudices. In this section, we work to further understand the role of racial considerations in shaping perceptions of social programs and their beneficiaries, again isolating on the role of spending mode in either activating or deactivating racialized thinking.

We begin by exploring preferences for the two programs outlined at the beginning of this chapter: TANF and the EITC. To do this, we turn to data from a subsample of one thousand respondents from the 2014 Cooperative Congressional Election Study.[48] The Common Content Module of the CCES asked respondents whether spending on welfare programs should be increased, kept about the same, or decreased.[49] This module of the CCES, using the same three-point scale, asked respondents for their preferred levels of spending for "tax breaks to help subsidize the incomes of low-wage earners"—a colloquial description for the EITC.

We use these responses to measure public support for direct (welfare) and tax-code (the EITC) spending on social welfare programs. Support for welfare spending is weaker than support for increasing spending on the EITC: 37 percent of respondents professed a desire to decrease welfare spending, while only 26 percent said that they wanted to increase it: the comparable numbers are 24 percent and 47 percent for the EITC, which is more popular than traditional welfare spending.

To measure racial attitudes, we employ an abridged version of the symbolic racism scale developed by P. J. Henry and David Sears.[50] We asked respondents for their level of agreement with two statements (on a five-point scale ranging from "strongly agree" to "strongly disagree"). The first was:

Table 5.5 Predicting Attitudes Toward Welfare and the Earned Income Tax Credit, 2014

	Welfare Spending Support		EITC Spending Support	
Symbolic racism	−0.15*	−0.08*	−0.12*	−0.04*
	(0.01)	(0.01)	(0.01)	(0.01)
Ideological self-identification		−0.00		−0.00
		(0.01)		(0.03)
Income		−0.03*		−0.03*
		(0.01)		(0.01)
Trust in government		0.06*		0.02
		(0.02)		(0.02)
Egalitarianism		0.13*		0.14*
		(0.02)		(0.01)
White		0.01		−0.04
		(0.07)		(0.08)
Male		−0.00		−0.00
		(0.05)		(0.06)
Constant	2.64*	1.47*	2.84*	1.77*
	(0.07)	(0.15)	(0.20)	(0.19)
N	763	676	756	673

Source: 2014 Cooperative Congressional Election Study.

Note: Estimates are seemingly unrelated regression estimates (robust standard errors in parentheses).

* $p < .05$

"Irish, Italians, Jewish, and many other minorities overcame prejudice and worked their way up. Blacks should do the same without any special favors." The second was: "Generations of slavery and discrimination have created conditions that make it difficult for blacks to work their way out of the lower class." Responses to these questions were added together (the second of the questions was reverse-coded) to create a scale of symbolic racism ranging from 0 to 8, with higher values indicating higher levels of symbolic racism.[51]

Do racial considerations predict attitudes toward these programs? Columns 1 and 3 of table 5.5 present results of seemingly unrelated regression models predicting welfare and EITC attitudes as a simple function of our symbolic racism scale. Consistent with what might be expected, the models show that support for both programs is negatively correlated with higher levels of symbolic racism: all else being equal, those who score at the highest value on the symbolic racism scale are roughly 1.5 points (on a three-point scale) less supportive of welfare spending, and roughly 1.2 points less supportive of EITC spending, than those at the lowest level of symbolic racism.

Figure 5.3 Expected Levels of Support for Welfare and EITC Spending, by Symbolic Racism Score, 2014

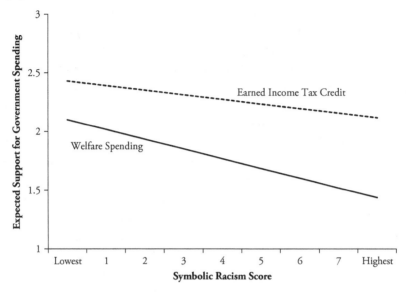

Source: 2014 Cooperative Congressional Election Study.

At least correlationally, racial attitudes are predictive of attitudes toward all manner of spending to help the less fortunate. Importantly, however, we see that the coefficient for the symbolic racism variable in the welfare spending model is larger than the coefficient in the EITC model (and the difference between these coefficients is statistically significant: $\chi^2 = 6.78$, $p < .01$). What this tells us is that welfare attitudes are more closely connected than EITC attitudes to racial considerations.

Columns 2 and 4 of table 5.5 add the individual covariates used in table 5.4 to these basic models. The inclusion of these variables does a good deal to diminish the independent effect of racial considerations for both types of spending, as racial prejudices are highly correlated with some of the other predictors (particularly egalitarianism). But the relative magnitude of the symbolic racism coefficient across spending types, if anything, becomes larger in the presence of these controls: once controls are added, the coefficient for symbolic racism is roughly twice what it is in the EITC model, a difference that is again statistically significant ($\chi^2 = 4.82$, $p < .05$).

Figure 5.3 provides an indicator of the substantive impact of these differences: showing respondents' expected level of support for welfare and

EITC spending as a function of symbolic racism, it holds the other variables constant at their mean values. Support for the EITC tends to be somewhat higher than support for welfare regardless of a respondent's symbolic racism score. But since symbolic racism matters more to attitudes toward welfare than it does for attitudes toward the EITC, the differences in relative levels of support for these two programs becomes greater as a respondent moves up the symbolic racism scale. For those highest in symbolic racism, the difference in relative levels of support for the two programs is roughly twice as large as it is for those scoring lowest.[52]

These results are generally consistent with our assertion that social benefits delivered through the tax code are less likely to prime racial considerations than benefits delivered through direct government spending. The existence of differences in the importance of racial attitudes in attitudes toward "real world" social spending programs is supportive of our expectations and sheds light on why, all else being equal, the EITC is more popular than welfare.

Of course, this finding has several limitations. Most importantly, welfare and the EITC are different programs with different target populations. Though it is important to keep in mind that (at least for the past twenty years) most direct government assistance programs for able-bodied adults have required that recipients are either working or searching for work, the EITC is explicitly targeted toward people who are already in the workforce. And of course, the word "welfare" itself is racially charged. It is certainly possible, then, that the EITC is less likely to activate racial considerations than welfare spending because it is explicitly designed to benefit the working poor—a group of people whom citizens almost by definition consider more "deserving" than the poor who are not working. In any case, it is clear that welfare and the EITC differ in ways that go well beyond the program delivery mechanism. To isolate the effects of delivery mechanism more directly, we return to the survey experimental approach.

Race, Spending Mode, and Low-Income Assistance

This experiment, which was conducted on a nationally representative sample during August 2016, uses vignettes similar to those constructed in chapter 4. Respondents were asked for their level of support (as measured on a 0–4 scale ranging from "strongly support" to "strongly oppose") for a hypothetical downwardly distributing social policy providing assistance to low-income citizens. As in chapter 4, aside from the delivery mechanism treatment, all other information about the program remained identical, allowing us to isolate the impact of delivery mechanism on program support. The wording for the two delivery mechanism frames are:

Direct spending: "Some have endorsed a program that would provide low-income citizens with assistance in paying for groceries and other necessities. Under this program, certain citizens would receive monthly checks from the government that could be used to purchase groceries and other necessities. The total cost of this program is expected to be $65 billion per year."

Tax expenditure: "Some have endorsed a program that would provide low-income citizens with assistance in paying for groceries and other necessities. Under this program, citizens who earn taxable income would be eligible to deduct the amount of money they pay for groceries from their taxable income. These tax credits would reduce the amount of federal income tax these citizens pay each year and can result in a citizen receiving a tax credit from the federal government instead of paying federal income taxes at all. The total cost of this program is expected to be $65 billion per year."

Columns 1 (direct spending) and 3 (tax expenditure) of table 5.6 show results predicting attitudes toward these programs as a function of the same two-question symbolic racism scale used in table 5.5. As in table 5.5, models are run separately for each spending frame using seemingly unrelated regression. And as in table 5.5, we see evidence that racial considerations are significantly ($\chi^2 = 4.20$, $p < .05$) more strongly predictive of attitudes toward this program when it is portrayed as a direct spending program than when it is portrayed as a tax expenditure program. Again, these results show that while symbolic racism depresses program support regardless of spending type, the impact of racial considerations is stronger for the direct spending frame.

Columns 2 and 4 add in the battery of demographic and political controls. These results, while again showing that support for social welfare programs goes well beyond racial considerations, further highlight how spending mode affects the relative impact of racial considerations. After controlling for other

Table 5.6 Americans' Attitudes Toward Social Welfare Spending as a Function of Spending Frame, 2016

	Direct Spending Frame		Tax Expenditure Frame	
Symbolic racism	−0.26*	−0.08*	−0.19*	−0.01
	(0.02)	(0.03)	(0.02)	(0.03)
Ideological self-identification		0.06		−0.01
		(0.04)		(0.05)
Income		−0.01		−0.05*
		(0.02)		(0.02)
Trust in government		0.34*		0.25*
		(0.08)		(0.09)
Egalitarianism		0.15*		0.20*
		(0.02)		(0.02)
White		0.19		0.05
		(0.10)		(0.13)
Male		0.12		0.10
		(0.11)		(0.12)
Constant	4.74*	1.63*	4.35*	1.29
	(0.12)	(0.41)	(0.02)	(0.41)
R^2	0.23	0.39	0.12	0.36
N	430	405	437	401

Source: YouGov survey, August 2016.

Note: Estimates are seemingly unrelated regression coefficients (standard errors in parentheses).

*$p < .05$

factors, the impact of symbolic racism on attitudes toward spending in the tax expenditure frame essentially goes to zero, while symbolic racism remains a substantively important predictor of attitudes in the direct spending frame. The difference in relative magnitude of these coefficients remains statistically significant ($\chi^2 = 4.79, p < .05$). As in table 5.1, trust in government also is a stronger predictor in the direct spending frame than in the tax expenditure frame, though the differences in coefficients across models is only marginally significant (ss models is only marginally = 2.63, $p < .10$).

Figure 5.4 gives a sense of the magnitude of these differences, showing expected support as a function of symbolic racism and spending frame type, again holding the other variables constant at their means. This figure illustrates that while the mean support for this program does not differ significantly by spending mode, racial attitudes strongly affect the type of spending that respondents would prefer: those lowest in symbolic racism are expected

Figure 5.4 Expected Levels of Support for Government Assistance, by Spending Type and Symbolic Racism Score, 2016

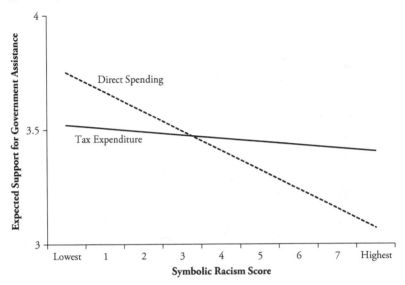

Source: YouGov survey, August 2016.

to prefer the direct spending program to the tax expenditure program, while those high in symbolic racism are expected to prefer the opposite. Again, the core implication is that direct spending programs activate racial considerations in a way that otherwise identical tax expenditures do not.

Race and the Deservingness of Beneficiaries

Finally, we circle back to the central goal of this section: understanding how racial considerations affect the perceived deservingness of government beneficiaries. To do so, we return to the vignettes, introduced earlier in the chapter, in which respondents were asked to rate the deservingness of six hypothetical recipients of government aid. This section has shown that spending mode plays a significant role in conditioning perceptions of deservingness: those who receive aid through the tax code were perceived as more deserving than those who receive it through direct means. We hypothesized that this difference in respondents' perceptions of recipients may be partly a function of the tax code frame's deemphasizing of racial considerations and of factors associated with racial considerations.

Figure 5.5 Standardized Impact of Symbolic Racism on Deservingness Perceptions, by Spending Mode, 2016

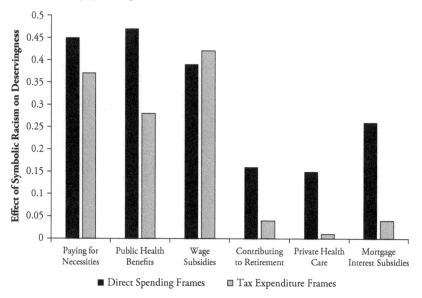

Source: YouGov survey, August 2016.
Note: Figure entries are standardized OLS regression coefficients.

To evaluate these hypotheses, we use the same two-question symbolic racism scale as earlier to predict deservingness perceptions in each of the six vignettes. Figure 5.5 illustrates the results of simple OLS regression models predicting deservingness perceptions as a function of symbolic racism. The figure displays standardized coefficients of the effect of symbolic racism on deservingness for each of the six vignettes, separated by spending frame.

The results show that, at least in this simple model, symbolic racism is strongly associated with perceptions of deservingness. These effects are typically strongest for the downwardly distributing programs, since these are the sorts of programs that, in the telling of Gilens and others, are the most likely to "code black" and thus conjure racially charged imagery in the minds of some respondents.[53] But for all six programs, symbolic racism is significantly ($p < .01$) associated with deservingness perceptions, with those higher in symbolic racism perceiving beneficiaries as less deserving than those low in symbolic racism.

Table 5.7 adds symbolic racism to the list of covariates used to predict deservingness in table 5.3 and segments out the results by spending mode

Table 5.7 Predicting the Deservingness of Government Aid Recipients, 2016

	Public Health Benefits		Assistance in Paying for Necessities		Wage Subsidies	
	Direct Spending Frame	Tax Expenditure Frame	Direct Spending Frame	Tax Expenditure Frame	Direct Spending Frame	Tax Expenditure Frame
Symbolic racism	-.06*	-.03	-.10*	-.05*	-.07*	-.08*
Ideology (liberal-conservative scale)	-.17*	-.03*	-.01	-.09*	-.09*	-.01
Education (highest degree earned)	-.01	-.00	-.08*	-.07*	.00	-.02
Family income	-.00	-.00	-.01	.03*	-.01	.00
Trust in government	.15*	.08	.14*	.12*	.11	.09
Egalitarianism	.09*	.08*	.10*	.08*	.07*	.12*
Race (white)	.15	.21*	.02	-.06	.06	.15*
Gender (female)	.15	-.06	.06	.07	.33*	.03
R^2	.39	.17	.31	.26	.27	.30
N	346	381	343	363	356	331

	Subsidized Retirement Savings		Subsidized Mortgage Benefits		Subsidized Private Health Benefits	
	Direct Spending Frame	Tax Expenditure Frame	Direct Spending Frame	Tax Expenditure Frame	Direct Spending Frame	Tax Expenditure Frame
Symbolic racism	.01	.00	-.06*	-.01	-.06*	-.00
Ideology (liberal-conservative scale)	.00	.03	-.00	.02	.07*	.03
Education (highest degree earned)	.00	.10*	.00	.03	.03	.02
Family income	-.01	.02	-.01	.02	-.02	.03*
Trust in government	.28*	.09	.17*	.12	.16*	.15*
Egalitarianism	.02	.11*	.02	-.03	-.01	-.01
Race (white)	-.33*	-.15	-.41*	.01	-.29*	-.28*
Gender (female)	.10	.02	-.02	.16	.17*	.17*
R^2	.09	.06	.10	.10	.07	.07
N	526	531	531	526	523	533

Source: YouGov survey, August 2016.

Note: Table entries are seemingly unrelated regression coefficients.

$*p < .05$

treatment. This table shows that the effect of symbolic racism on deserving-ness perceptions—as well as the relative importance of symbolic racism across spending modes—is generally robust to a variety of statistical controls. Even after taking into account factors like ideology and egalitarianism, for example, we still see that symbolic racism does more of the work in predicting deservingness perceptions of recipients of direct spending than it does with recipients of tax expenditures.

Conclusion

In this chapter, we have worked to unpack why tax expenditure programs are more popular than direct spending programs, focusing on the ways in which spending mode conditions how citizens think about the recipients of government aid. Given that tax expenditure programs are reasonably considered more likely to prime the positively valanced term "taxpayer" (and direct spending programs are more likely to prime the negatively valenced "government aid recipient"), we expected, and found, that people who receive aid through the tax code are perceived as more deserving than people who receive otherwise identical aid directly. This happens, at least in part, because tax expenditure spending also serves to dampen some of the racialized thinking often associated with "recipients of government aid."

These results, of course, come with limitations. First and perhaps most importantly, all of the social benefits that we presented to respondents are benefits that are available in some form in the real world. In the first set of analyses, we did this by design in order to understand attitudes toward welfare and the EITC specifically. But in the other experiments, the issues that respondents were asked to consider were ones with which they may have had some direct or indirect experience—for example, purchasing health insurance through a government program or receiving assistance in purchasing day-to-day necessities.

Though most citizens are unfamiliar with the details of federal policy programs, our experimental results may be affected to some extent by citizens' actual experiences or perceptions of how these sorts of social benefits are delivered. To use one of the vignettes from our third analysis as an example, a "federal tax credit for low-wage work" does exist in the real world, but a "monthly payment to supplement low-wage work" does not. It would be useful in the future to replicate these results in areas where the federal government currently plays a less visible role—such as paid family leave or universal pre-K education—to see whether the delivery mechanism also has an impact on attitudes toward programs that are purely hypothetical.

Despite these limitations, our results have a number of implications for the study of public opinion and the American welfare state. Our results suggest that the public finds social tax expenditures, all else being equal, more palatable than direct social spending programs. This preference has multiple causes, but it is driven at least in part by the structure of benefit delivery, which affects how citizens perceive beneficiaries. The preference for tax expenditures also helps to explain why policymakers have turned to helping low-income workers through the EITC and away from traditional welfare: besides delivering benefits in a different way, a social tax expenditure program also provides cues that lead some citizens to think that it delivers benefits to more deserving beneficiaries than benefits delivered directly by government.

More broadly speaking, our results from the past two chapters show that the social construction of actual or potential beneficiaries of government aid is not fully exogenous to government programs themselves; instead, it is influenced by the design of public policy. Public policies tend to earn popular support when their beneficiaries are perceived as deserving. But we argue that a policy design can bestow certain virtues (such as deservingness) on a target group, thus explaining in part why political parties work to target government spending at electoral constituencies that are less popular with the general public. For policymakers seeking to reduce inequality, then, tax expenditures may have one critical advantage over direct spending programs: they help to frame their recipients in a way that in all likelihood makes the spending to benefit them more politically feasible. In our concluding chapter, we revisit this idea of feasibility, examining the role—and possible downsides—of spending through the tax code as a way to address the issues of income inequality and opportunity in the United States.

CHAPTER 6

The Public and the Private Welfare State

THE GOAL OF this book has been to advance the understanding of public opinion toward social spending by examining attitudes about social tax subsidies. We have shown that social tax expenditures, almost regardless of their intent or redistributive effects, are popular, and we argue that this broad-based popularity is due at least in part to pairing a delivery mechanism that appeals to moderates and conservatives with the financing of social goals that are popular across the political spectrum. The policy design of the tax expenditure comports well with a "symbolically conservative, operationally liberal" citizenry: Americans are skeptical of "government" in a broad sense, but also supportive of mechanisms to deliver social benefits to citizens. By delivering money indirectly, through private firms and markets, tax expenditures can fulfill public demands for both an active government role in particular policy areas and a smaller, less intrusive government. One implication of our findings is that how the federal government delivers social benefits can move the subset of the population who are skeptical of government toward supporting more spending.

In addition, tax expenditures are particularly popular compared to direct spending among people who might otherwise be skeptical of government intervention (Republicans, conservatives, those with low levels of trust in government). We have demonstrated that citizens with antigovernment attitudes who are generally not supportive of direct social spending are nevertheless supportive of a range of social tax expenditure programs. The uptick in support from groups that generally are against federal spending is one reason for the high popularity level of social tax expenditures. Moreover, the delivery of social spending through the tax code does not depress support among groups that are less antigovernment, such as liberals, egalitarians, and Democrats. Our findings suggest that examining attitudes toward policies funded through other policy tools, such as grants, loans, and government corporations, may produce systematic variations in support that are closer to support for social tax expenditures and less reflective of factors that influence direct spending programs. Given the growing use of these alternative policy tools, our explanation for public opinion toward tax expenditures may become more relevant in understanding the impact of attitudes on changes to federal spending in the future.

Next, we find that tax expenditure programs also help to mute some of the racial stereotyping and opinions about "undeservingness" that undergird much opposition to social welfare spending in the United States. Americans have long cast lower-income citizens, for example, into categories of "deserving" or "undeserving," and who they want to help through social policy and who they do not is determined to some extent by those perceptions.[1] A tax credit can do some of the work of convincing people that a particular beneficiary is "deserving" in a way that a direct payment cannot: by connoting that benefits go only to the normatively valued category of "taxpayer," credits can send the signal that beneficiaries are hardworking citizens and thus deserving of aid.[2] This logic extends to the interaction between social tax expenditures and the racial considerations Americans bring to evaluating federal social spending. We demonstrate that social welfare delivered through the tax code does not prime racial bias in evaluations of social spending to the same degree as benefits delivered through direct programs. Scholars have long shown that social perceptions of potential beneficiaries of government aid play a strong role in determining how government can spend its money. We find here that the reverse is also at least partly true: a policy's construction and design affect what citizens think about its beneficiaries.

We have presented evidence that social tax expenditures are not "invisible" to Americans and that beneficiaries of these programs report strong support for spending through the tax code. We argue that social tax expenditure recipients have multiple ways to learn about their eligibility for these benefits through their employer and also through the involved process of annually filing federal income tax returns. We demonstrate that recipients of social tax expenditures are more aware of their status as a government beneficiary than previously reported. We asked survey respondents whether or not they personally had benefited from a government subsidy and compared their answers to their use of both social tax expenditure and direct social programs. Our results show that changing the question wording slightly from "government social programs" (the wording used in the 2011 Mettler analysis) to "government subsidies" increased the awareness of social tax expenditure beneficiaries that they had benefited from the government. This finding indicates that some respondents are responding to the distinction between benefiting from social benefits and benefiting from subsidies, although in reality all are recipients of federal aid. These results are further supported by our analysis showing that respondents who were eligible for a social tax expenditure program were more supportive of the same program compared to respondents who did not qualify for it, all else being equal. In fact, the variable representing economic self-interest is the strongest predictor for support of social tax expenditures across six different programs. And since social tax expenditure beneficiaries are wealthier and more educated than the average voter, it may be politically difficult to directly reduce or eliminate these programs without risking a backlash from a group of citizens who donate, volunteer, and vote.

Finally, we demonstrate that traditional factors normally taken into account by citizens when they form preferences for direct social spending, such as partisanship and ideology, do not extend to social tax expenditures. We argue that social tax expenditures, by design, are difficult to politicize. Our analysis finds that partisanship, ideology, and political values such as individualism are not consistent predictors of support for social tax subsidies. For example, while Republican respondents were less likely than Democrats to support the EITC, they were not more likely to support programs such as the Home Mortgage Interest Deduction or deductions for 401(k)s and IRAs. Political values that in the past have been reliable predictors of support for direct social programs, such as egalitarianism, do not correlate with higher levels of support for social tax expenditures. We conclude from our analysis that the conflicting political cues from the tax break and social welfare components of a social tax expenditure description lead respondents either to default to personal economic interest or to rely on their perceptions of recipients to evaluate these programs. An implication of our analysis is that citizens' ability to translate their political beliefs into government spending preferences depends on the method of delivery.

The Popularity of Regressive Tax Expenditures and Rising Economic Inequality

Most major U.S. social tax expenditure programs, as currently constructed, have ostensibly universal goals, such as homeownership and retirement security, but tend to benefit the wealthy. Such programs remain popular despite redistributive effects that citizens might not find palatable in part because they are delivered through the tax code rather than through direct payments. As a result, many tax expenditures, even those that regressively redistribute wealth, are difficult to change. Serving as an advantage for those policymakers who wish to protect existing tax expenditure programs, even highly regressive ones, is the fact that such programs are viewed in a more positive light than they would be if the same benefits were delivered through direct payments. The immense popularity of social tax expenditures, especially for cross-pressured voters, contributes to a divided social welfare state that does as much to increase income inequality as it does to reduce it.

The resulting difficulty in reforming tax policy has been felt by both Democratic and Republican administrations. Two major reform efforts have been made in the last decade—one addressing health care under a Democratic administration and the other tackling tax policy during a Republican presidency. In both cases, major tax expenditures were put on the table as items that could be cut in exchange for new policies or benefits. But in both cases the social tax expenditures survived, and some were even expanded. The fact that even progressive presidents have added to or resisted challenging entrenched tax expenditure programs speaks to the high level of support for such programs.

The 2009 health care reform effort put everything on the table to be amended, including eliminating or replacing the popular tax exclusion for employment-based health care (a program known to distort the health insurance market and therefore detested by economists). The final version of Obamacare not only did not touch the employment-based health care exclusion—which, again, provides benefits only to those whose employers offer health benefits—but added a number of new health care tax credits for employers and employees alike to be used on the newly created health insurance market.

These sorts of concerns extend to areas beyond health care. In 2015, President Obama proposed an ambitious universal pre-K program and promised that it would be paid for by eliminating the 529 plan tax expenditure program that helps largely wealthy families save for college. Democrats Nancy Pelosi and Chris Van Hollen lobbied the president to kill his proposal because of the potential backlash of suburban voters to cutting the popular program. The Democratic Party's coalition is made up of working-class minorities and wealthier suburban and urban liberals. It is unclear if wealthier liberals within the Democratic Party are willing to support an expansion of public welfare programs tilted toward the poor at the expense of social tax expenditures that they use to subsidize their own family's health care insurance and their children's college expenses. The socioeconomic diversity of the Democratic Party's electoral coalition places a limit on members' efforts to reduce inequality through changes to social welfare spending.

President Trump and congressional Republicans passed the Tax Cuts and Jobs Act (TCJA) in 2017. Republicans hailed the new law as a landmark piece of tax reform that would grow the economy. Not only did President Trump promise to protect popular social tax expenditures like the 401(k) deduction, but paradoxically, he claimed that the new law would "dramatically simplify the tax code." House Speaker Paul Ryan promised that the TCJA would "[throw] out the special-interest loopholes that riddle the code."[3] In fact, the overall number of federal tax expenditures increased from 293 in 2017 to 298 in 2018.[4] Moreover, a number of new social tax subsidies were included in the TCJA, such as a tax credit for family and medical leave, a deduction for higher education expenses, and a personal exemption for children.

However, there were changes to marginal income tax rates and the standard deduction that are expected to reduce the value of some social tax expenditure programs over time. And while the TCJA reduced the benefit of some individual social tax expenditure programs, it did not reduce the overall regressive impact of social tax expenditures as a group. The Congressional Budget Office estimated that the new law would cost

$1.5 trillion over the next decade and mainly help corporations and wealthier families through provisions such as changes to the alternative minimum tax and income from pass-through businesses. The large corporate tax cuts reduced the progressivity of the federal tax system. And although the lower marginal rates and higher standard deduction reduced the value of many regressive social tax expenditures, the wealthiest taxpayers still receive more benefits from these programs than do middle- and working-class families.[5] So even with dramatic changes to the system of federal taxes that reduced the value of regressive tax expenditures and added several tax credits, the overall impact of social tax expenditures is to distribute federal revenues up the income ladder.

However, the doubling of the standard deduction in the TCJA will reduce the number of households who itemize their federal tax returns. Tax experts are projecting that the percentage of itemizers will drop from 30 to 10 percent of all taxpayers in the next decade.[6] And the taxpayers who will stop itemizing their annual returns are from middle-class and upper-middle-class households, leaving only the rich to itemize their tax returns. Doubling the standard deduction and lowering marginal income tax rates reduces both the number of people who will claim itemized deductions and the value of existing tax expenditures to households. If fewer households itemize their returns, then support for social tax subsidies could erode over time as these programs become truly just welfare for the wealthy.

Tax Expenditures as a Vehicle to Expand Social Welfare for the Working Poor

As currently constituted, most major tax expenditures distribute benefits upward. But fully refundable social tax expenditures need not be regressive.[7] One could imagine a number of programs that might provide benefits to lower-income Americans—an expansion of the EITC, the growth or expansion of tax credits for child care, pre-K tuition, and the like, or even a tax credit for renters. We have demonstrated in this book that, because of how tax expenditures are delivered, they are particularly apt to appeal to those Americans who like spending on popular social goals but are also distrustful of government and often skeptical of beneficiaries of government assistance, and who believe strongly that individuals should help themselves. That tax expenditure programs seem to achieve both goals—a limited government and a strong system of social benefits—suggests that they have a built-in "framing advantage" in that it is easier for policymakers to persuade the public to support private rather than public solutions to social problems. Direct social spending, by contrast, fulfills public demands for more social services but conflicts with public impulses to cut taxes and limit government, suggesting that, at the margins, those in favor of privatizing social services through tax expenditure policy should have an easier time mobilizing public support for their plans, especially if these programs are pitted against similar programs to be financed through direct means.

A tax credit also might limit the impact of racial biases on evaluations of federal social spending on the poor. In 2016, racially resentful Americans flocked to the campaign of Donald Trump.[8] But as it turned out, many of these same Americans also supported a larger federal role in spending on social welfare programs. As the country's demographics change, white American backlash against government spending on programs perceived to be used mainly by people of color will grow. The relative difference in favorability between direct and indirect spending is one of the reasons why welfare and food stamps have been contracting over the last four decades while the Earned Income Tax Credit has grown. A policymaker who wants to target government assistance to the poor in a way that does not risk white backlash may be more successful offering a tax credit than a more direct government program.

There are limits to how much an expansion of refundable tax credits can be used to reduce poverty in the United States. First, the major refundable credits are skewed toward assistance to families and provide little support to childless adults.[9] The stagnation of wages for men with only a high school degree is a persistent problem in the United States: these refundable credits do nothing to augment their low wages. Second, the EITC has a phase-in structure that provides fewer benefits to poorer recipients. Third, refundable tax credits do not reward unpaid labor, such as child rearing, or provide any assistance to those who are unemployed. Refundable tax credits, unlike direct cash-equivalent aid, are not countercyclical to downturns in the economy, so they are less useful during economic recessions. And perhaps most importantly, claiming many tax expenditures requires the active participation of those who are eligible. If they do not take the steps to begin the process, they may not get the benefit to which they are entitled, undercutting the purpose of having the tax credit codified into law in the first place. The Internal Revenue Service, for example, notes that roughly 20 percent of households that are eligible for the Earned Income Tax Credit do not claim it on their tax returns.[10] The percentage of unclaimed tax credits is lower for mortgage interest, student loan interest, and similar programs, but tax expenditures designed to distribute income downward more often go unclaimed simply because potential claimants are less likely to have the knowledge or resources to deal with a complex tax system. So while refundable tax credits are politically popular and sustainable ways to assist the working poor, there are some real limitations in such programs.

Even so, policymakers interested in expanding assistance for lower-income Americans still view tax expenditures as an integral part of their plans. Candidates for the Democratic Party's 2020 presidential nomination introduced a number of new social tax expenditure programs that may have provided a preview of new tax expenditures for the working poor and families to come. Democratic senator Cory Booker of New Jersey proposed the American Opportunity Accounts Act, a program that would create a tax-free savings account for every child at birth, with funds in the account becoming available when they turn eighteen. Senator Kamala Harris (D-CA) proposed the LIFT the Middle-Class Act, based on a yearly $6,000 tax credit for middle-class families. This tax credit would be unique in that it could be accessed at the end of each month in installments of up to $500 for each family and $250 for individuals. In addition, a number of candidates pushed for expansions to the Earned Income Tax Credit and new and expanded tax credits to assist with child care costs and job training. Democratic senator Kirsten Gillibrand of New York proposed nearly tripling the dependent and child care tax credit to a maximum of $6,000. This plan would also make the child care tax credit available to parents who are part-time students. Gillibrand also suggested a plan that would subsidize, through the tax code, businesses that help their employees find affordable child care. Senator Amy Klobuchar (D-MN) proposed the Middle-Class Opportunity Act, which would support expanding the dependent and child care tax credit and provide additional credits for higher education and assistance for aging parents. If some of these plans for working families and child care become law, then we would expect support for spending through the tax code (driven by self-interest) to extend to families with young children and to working-class adults.

Some candidates made proposals that recognized the disproportionate advantages that the current tax code gives to homeowners as compared to renters. Senators Harris and Booker proposed new tax credits just for renters. Booker's tax credit would help low-income renters who spend more than 30 percent of their income on housing, which would include rent and utilities. In his plan, renters would receive the difference between their rental payment and 30 percent of their monthly adjusted gross income. In addition, renters could defer 20 percent of their tax credit to a rainy-day fund that would help with unexpected future expenses. Senator Harris's proposed tax credit is similar, although targeted at households earning under $100,000. These new programs would put renters on par with home-owners in being able to access federal subsidies from the tax code. At a minimum, our analysis suggests that proposals to increase the number and scope of tax expenditures to help the working poor and low-income families would not meet the same resistance as direct spending programs designed to do the same thing: we would expect that American citizens would simply not politicize such programs in the same way. Also, renters would join homeowners in supporting tax expenditures that specifically applied to their housing situation.

Of course, one could argue that tax credits for low-income citizens are not as political as similar direct spending programs only because politicians have not yet chosen to politicize them. If we enter a world where the two parties decided to take highly polarized positions on programs like the Earned Income Tax Credit (or on upwardly distributing programs, such as the mortgage interest deduction), it would be natural to expect partisans to follow suit. The way issues "newly" introduced into the political system become rapidly polarized once elite parties decide to diverge on them suggests that tax expenditure polarization could work the same way. We argue, however, that unlike other sorts of new social programs, elite-level polarization on tax expenditures is unlikely, or at least less likely, to happen. At the elite level, tax expenditure programs provide ways for both parties to get something they want—an expanded social welfare state for Democrats, a smaller amount of federal tax revenue for Republicans. They also provide ways for both parties to send important signals to cross-pressured or ambivalent voters: Democrats can credibly claim that they are lowering taxes and reducing the reach of the federal government, while Republicans can credibly claim that they are offering assistance to those who need it and deserve it. Because of these factors, those seeking to reduce inequality or provide a stronger social safety net might productively look to the tax code as a way to do it.

The Future of Public Attitudes Toward Social Spending in America

There are significant changes occurring to the nation and the economy that promise to alter Americans' public attitudes toward social spending. In this section, we outline promising areas of future research related to public opinion toward the divided American welfare state. One such study could contribute to the policy feedback literature by examining how the use of social tax expenditures alters public opinion toward direct social spending programs. One of our major findings is that respondents who were eligible for benefits through the tax code were strongly supportive of social tax expenditure programs. We would expect these same respondents to be less supportive of public social programs. For example, a citizen who is enrolled in employment-based health care insurance and receives the accompanying tax exclusion can be expected to be less supportive of a Medicare-for-all proposal that eliminates private health insurance compared to someone with no health insurance through an employer.

Citizens' reliance on one side of the divided welfare state versus the other reflects their relative preferences for direct spending versus social tax subsidies. There is a socioeconomic class and political power aspect of this divide: middle-class and wealthier households use social tax expenditures for private insurance, while lower-income families, and especially racial and ethnic minorities, are more reliant on the public side.[11] If there is a socioeconomic class bias in the American policymaking process, then wealthier households' preferences for social tax expenditures might be better received and acted upon by policymakers than demands from working-class families for direct social welfare programs.[12] However, the notion of a socioeconomic bias in American policymaking is disputed.[13] Our own results show that public sentiment favors a mode of spending that is most commonly used to distribute money to wealthier citizens. The enigma of the American welfare state is that there are more programs assisting more households than commonly realized, but most of this social assistance does little to redistribute income and assuage rising inequality.

As the country becomes more racially and ethnically diverse, the racialization of opinion toward social welfare policies is likely to intensify and become an even more important issue in determining the political sustainability of programs for the poor. In our analysis, we discovered that racially resentful respondents were more accepting of social tax expenditure programs for the working poor than they were of identical programs described as direct spending programs. A next step in the research of attitudes toward social tax subsidies is to examine how white identity influences preferences for different types of social spending. Two findings in our analysis point to the possibility of a relationship between Americans with higher levels of white identity and support for social tax subsidies. First, white Americans were positively (but not always statistically significantly) more supportive of social tax expenditures. This pattern of white Americans' support for tax subsidies, combined with the established findings that racially resentful whites disapprove of public welfare, may point to a racial division for different types of social spending. We find that racially resentful Americans evaluate social tax subsidies more favorably compared to identical direct social programs. It should be noted, however, that white identity is a different concept than racial resentment.[14] Americans who score high on a white identity scale may favor social tax subsidies because they assume that these programs disproportionately help white families at the expense of racial minorities who are assisted on the public side of the divided welfare state.

The most significant predictor of support for expanded social tax expenditures is whether or not a respondent is eligible for the program. The expansion of the standard deduction under the TCJA will result in fewer taxpayers claiming major social credits and deductions. The logic here is simple. If more taxpayers over time form the habit of just claiming the standard deduction, then they will no longer be involved in claiming individual social tax expenditure benefits such as the Home Mortgage Interest Deduction or the charitable contribution deduction. A taxpayer who no longer annually claims social tax benefits will lose personal interest in supporting this type of spending and may even become resentful, for not only do they not personally benefit from these programs, but the only recipients of their benefits will be the wealthiest of American families. If the average middle-class family no longer receives an annual tax statement from their bank on their home mortgage interest or decides to stop itemizing their charitable contributions, then they may no longer consider the tax code a vehicle for personal benefits. If the TCJA changes stick, then not only will fewer families claim social tax benefits, but those who do will be firmly in the top 1 percent—thus opening up these programs to new political attacks.

As we write the concluding chapter of this book, America is experiencing a global pandemic due to the spread of COVID-19 and a worldwide recession. The federal government passed emergency measures that drastically changed the U.S. social safety net. First, the federal government created for the first time federal sick leave for anyone seeking or receiving treatment related to the novel coronavirus for two weeks at full pay. Second, the federal government, also for the first time, created a national paid family leave policy for up to twelve weeks for those caring for children whose schools or day cares are closed. Third, the federal government made direct payments to people affected by mass shutdowns due to the pandemic. Fourth, there was a massive expansion of federal unemployment insurance, in terms of both eligibility and benefits. These changes might last only through the current crisis, but once benefits are entrenched in the political system, they are difficult to scale back. The framing around federal social benefits has changed from addressing rising inequality to combating the effects of a global health pandemic. It is hard to say at this point whether the window for a drastic expansion of direct social programs is opening or politics will revert to some type of pre-coronavirus equilibrium.

The political effects of a pandemic resulting in an economic recession or depression could exacerbate existing trends in employment-based social insurance and benefits. The major federal tax expenditures are tied to workplace benefits. These tax subsidies have supported the U.S. claim to being the largest private welfare state in the world.[15] In the economic shutdown of April 2020, over 35 million American workers lost both their job and their health insurance. And employment-based social benefits were already trending down in previous years, in both the number of workers claiming them and fiscal generosity. In the post-pandemic economy, global market pressures may reduce corporations' incentives to provide benefits to middle-class employees' health care insurance and pension plans. In addition, an increase in automation and online work could reduce both the number of overall jobs and the number of jobs with employment-based benefits.

As part-time gig work, self-employment, and service jobs increase, a lower percentage of the labor force will be offered employment-base health care, pensions, and other types of benefits. We have shown here the importance of economic self-interest in support for social tax subsidies. If fewer workers are offered and enrolled in company benefits, will this translate into lower levels of support for federal social tax subsidies? Is it wise for a country to tie health care insurance to employment when a health pandemic can also shut down an economy? These questions will have to be addressed as the United States and the world build new safety nets for emerging challenges.

In general, however, we imagine that finding widespread support for any social programs designed to directly remediate the effects of growing income inequality will be extremely challenging in the current political climate. Republicans and conservatives oppose them on principle, and Democrats and liberals will have difficulty selling them to a public that increasingly does not trust government to do what is right. As Hetherington and Rudolph's aptly titled "Why Washington Won't Work" points out, there is simply little appetite in a polarized, distrustful environment for such programs to succeed.[16] Spending money through the tax code may provide a modest way forward in this sort of environment: tax expenditures combine elements of liberal and conservative thinking on social policy in a way that lessens the direct role of government in providing benefits and rewards citizens for engaging in private behaviors considered socially desirable. To date, most major tax expenditures have been vehicles for regressively redistributing wealth, one of the reasons that a wide range of policy scholars view them with some skepticism. But some recent proposals and the success of programs such as the EITC suggest that such expenditures can be used to expand economic opportunity and provide security for the less well-off. Global economic conditions portend inequality rising even further in the future, with all of its attendant social consequences. This issue—called by President Obama in 2011 the "defining issue of our time"—is one to which governments have been forced to respond.[17] In an era of partisan gridlock and social divisions, tax expenditures could provide one important way forward to augmenting low-income work, lowering the costs associated with raising a family, and narrowing the inequality gap.

NOTES

Chapter 1: Public Opinion Toward the Hidden Welfare State

1. Piketty 2014; Gottschalk and Danziger 2005; Hacker, Rehm, and Schlesinger 2013.
2. Telford 2019.
3. Kelly and Enns 2010; Enns and Wlezien 2011; Erikson, MacKuen, and Stimson 2002; Brooks and Manza 2008; McCall and Kenworthy 2009; Wlezien 2004.
4. On public concern about inequality, see, for example, Condon and Wichowsky 2020; Page and Jacobs 2009. On public support for direct government action to address inequality and lack of economic opportunity, see Brooks and Manza 2013; Kelly 2020.
5. Faricy 2015; Howard 1997; Hacker 2002; Mettler 2011; Morgan and Campbell 2011.
6. Howard 1997; Burman, Geissler, and Toder 2008.
7. Surrey 1974.
8. Rubin and Collins 2014.
9. Congressional Budget Office 2016.
10. For important exceptions, see Haselswerdt and Bartels 2015; Mettler 2011; Faricy and Ellis 2014; and Ashok and Huber 2019.
11. Hacker 2002; Howard 1997; Mettler 2011.
12. Mettler 2011.
13. Mettler 2011.
14. Mettler 2011, 37.
15. See, for example, Mayhew 1974; Levitt and Snyder 1997; and Stein and Bickers 1997.
16. Lazarus and Reilly 2010.
17. Egan 2013.
18. Faricy 2015.
19. Rubin 2012.
20. Ahearn 2007.
21. Delli Carpini and Keeter 1996; Achen and Bartels 2016; Key 1961.

22. Zaller 1992.
23. Free and Cantril 1969; Ellis and Stimson 2012.
24. Feldman 1988.
25. Ellis and Stimson 2012.
26. Mason 2018.
27. First, workers who are offered and enroll in employment-based social programs are made aware of these benefits at the time of their hiring and throughout the course of their employment from human resource departments, information from their paychecks, and annual reports on changes to their health care and pension plans. There is no shortage of information enabling workers to make the simple connection that they are invested in and benefit from employment-based health insurance, pension plans, and other social benefits. Second, citizens must consciously claim tax subsidies annually when they complete their tax returns. A citizen must enter information on their tax forms (or provide this information to an accountant or software program) on their home mortgage interest payments, property taxes, student loan interest, charitable contributions, IRA contributions, and medical expenses, to name a few. This process reminds citizens each and every year about which activities (homeownership, employment benefits, charitable contributions, and so on) are associated with federal tax subsidies and which are not. And often they can claim these tax benefits for years, if not decades, because they subsidize financial commitments such as paying off a home mortgage or student loans.
28. Slothuus 2007; van Oorschot 2006.
29. Van Oorschot 2000.
30. Gilens 1999; Piston 2018.
31. Morgan and Campbell 2011.
32. Pierson 1994.
33. The YouGov surveys were conducted using methods similar to those used in conducting the Cooperative Congressional Election Survey (CCES). YouGov is an online survey firm that recruits respondents to participate in surveys from a national panel. The YouGov panel uses a variety of means to recruit panelists, who are randomly invited to complete particular surveys as part of their participation. Panelists for the survey are recruited to be representative of the American public based on race, gender, age, geographical region, and education. For more information about YouGov's methods and a comparison to more traditional survey methods based on random-digit dialing, see Twyman 2008.

Chapter 2: The Politics of Private Social Welfare

1. This study examines only individual and household tax expenditures, not tax expenditures designed to benefit corporations.
2. Surrey 1974. Some conservative lawmakers reject the concept of tax expenditures on the ground that categorizing uncollected taxes as an expenditure assumes that all income belongs to the government (Howard 1997). For example, Republican senator Orin Hatch publicly rejected the JCT's concept of tax expenditures and offered his

own definition of such expenditures as "an opportunity for family and business to keep more of their income" (Faricy 2015).

3. Kiel and Eisenger 2018.
4. Office of Management and Budget 2019; Joint Committee on Taxation 2019.
5. Organization for Economic Cooperation and Development 2020.
6. Van Kersbergen and Vis 2014.
7. Organization for Economic Cooperation and Development 2010.
8. Faricy 2015.
9. Ibid.
10. Ibid.
11. Teles 2007.
12. Prasad 2018.
13. Stuerle 2000.
14. Ibid.
15. On moving some of Medicare to the private sector, see Morgan and Campbell 2011.
16. Faricy 2015.
17. EBRI 2016
18. Social Security Administration 2017.
19. Wolff 2013.
20. Department of Housing and Urban Development 2018.
21. Eastman and Tyger 2019.
22. Federal Reserve 2019.
23. Kaiser Family Foundation 2019; Reno and Walker 2019.
24. Mettler and Stonecash 2008.
25. Salamon 1989.
26. Converse 1964.
27. Hetherington 2005.
28. Piston 2018.
29. See, for example, Gilens 1999.

Chapter 3: Attitudes Toward Social Tax Expenditures

1. The order in which respondents received tax break questions was randomized.
2. See, for example, Jacoby 1994 and Goren 2008.
3. McCall 2013.
4. Chait 2011.
5. Williamson 2017.
6. Bartels 2016; Claggett and Schafer 2010.
7. McClelland and Airi 2020.
8. On meritocracy, see Hochschild 1981. On the tolerance of Americans for inequality, see Page and Jacobs 2009; Bartels 2016. Spencer Piston (2018) discusses Americans' resentment of the wealthy, and Christopher Ellis (2017) explores the belief that income earners in the top 1 percent are wealthy because of luck or circumstances of birth.
9. Mettler 2011.

10. One example of the question wording is: "Thinking about the money that the government spends on Social Security benefits, do you think that: most benefits of this spending go to upper-income citizens, most benefits of this spending go to middle-income citizens, or most benefits of this spending go to poorer citizens."

11. There are some perhaps expected partisan differences in responses: Democrats, for example, were significantly more likely than Republicans to say that the mortgage interest and retirement tax breaks distribute wealth upward.

12. See, for example, Carsey and Layman 2006; Mondak 1993; Hansen 1998; Busemeyer 2009; Mason 2018; Iyengar and Westwood 2015.

13. Eismeier 1982; Egan 2013.

14. In addition, Americans may resolve the ideological ambiguity of social welfare tax subsidies by focusing on whether the program is presented in ideological or group-specific language. Research shows that Republicans and Democrats discuss and frame policies in different terms: Republicans present policies as a means to advance a conservative agenda, and Democrats campaign on policies that target specific groups in society (Grossmann and Hopkins 2016). A citizen evaluating a federal program that directly targets money to a particular group may categorize the spending as "liberal" regardless of whether it is delivered as a direct check or a tax subsidy. The major social tax expenditure programs were in the tax code for decades before the rise of political polarization and were often legislated with no partisan debate (Howard 1997). No one program or set of social tax subsidies is owned by one political party or the other. And in contrast to public welfare, if there is any partisan association with social tax expenditures, it may be with the Republican Party. Republican leaders since Ronald Reagan have offered federal tax subsidies as solutions to a wide range of problems, from affordable health insurance to saving for retirement and even to disaster relief. Faricy (2015) shows that Republican Party control of the federal government has continually resulted in higher levels of social tax expenditures, and often at the expense of cuts to public social spending. The Republican Party has also made lowering federal taxes the centerpiece of its domestic agenda.

15. Funk 2000; Henderson and Hillygus 2011; Fong 2001.

16. Henderson et al. 1995.

17. Morgan and Campbell 2011.

18. As Mettler (2011) points out, whether they then take the next step—recognizing that these programs are a form of "government spending"—is another matter.

19. Mettler 2011.

20. Ibid.

21. Jacoby 2006. On values, see Rokeach 1973.

22. See, for example, McClosky and Zaller 1984; Achterberg, Houtman, and Derks 2011; Svallfors 2013.

23. Feldman and Steenbergen 2001.

24. Esping-Andersen 1990.

25. Attitudes toward the actual beneficiaries of particular programs are likely to play a role here as well. We return to this issue in chapter 4.

26. To measure "self-interest" for the low-wage tax credit, we simply use a measure of income. Other types of measures (for example, dummy variables for those who are

employed and earn a wage that would make them eligible for the Earned Income Tax Credit) yield similar results.

27. One complication here is that, since the passage of the Tax Cuts and Jobs Act of 2017, the size of the standard deduction has been increased, and many people who previously were able to itemize mortgage interest no longer do so. We conducted a pilot study of these self-interest indicators on the 2016 Cooperative Congressional Election Study. Though not all of the variables included in this survey were included on that one, and thus a full replication of these results is not possible, we find that, if anything, the importance of owning a home on support for the mortgage interest tax deduction was stronger in 2016 than it was in our 2019 survey.

28. Feldman and Steenbergen 2001.

29. As a check to make sure that the self-interest variables were measuring what we intended them to measure, we also ran a series of models that included "wrong" self-interest indicators for each of the tax expenditure programs (for example, predicting support for the mortgage interest deduction as a function of whether a respondent received health care through their employer). These variables were almost always insignificant and unimportant, giving us some confidence that our self-interest indicators are measuring experiences with the programs themselves, not generalized life circumstances that might be correlated with such experiences.

30. Mettler 2011.

Chapter 4: Tax Expenditures and Direct Spending: A Comparison

1. Jacoby 2000; Stimson 2016.
2. Cantril and Cantril 1999.
3. Free and Cantril 1964; Ellis and Stimson 2012.
4. Popp and Rudolph 2011; see also Silver and Pickett 2015; Claassen, Tucker, and Smith 2015; Johnston, Lavine, and Federico 2017.
5. Jacoby 2000.
6. Page and Jacobs 2009; Williamson 2017.
7. Sears and Citrin 1985; Dalton 2015.
8. Alesina and Glaeser 2004.
9. Hetherington 2005.
10. Jacoby 2000.
11. Ellis and Stimson 2012.
12. Soroka and Wlezien 2010.
13. Howard 1997.
14. Hacker 2002.
15. Mettler 2010.
16. Other recent experimental work supports this expectation. Haselswerdt and Bartels (2015) find, for example, that citizens were more supportive of a grant to help individuals buy housing when the program was framed as a "tax savings" as opposed to a "government grant."
17. Respondents were randomized separately into frames for each policy area, and the order in which respondents received the policy areas was also randomized. Questions

from five of the six policy areas were asked in our August 2014 survey—with replications for two areas run in a July 2017 survey to ensure that the results did not change over time—and questions from one, "green energy," were asked in August 2016.

18. Jacoby 2000; Rudolph and Evans 2005.

19. In another iteration of this experiment, performed on a convenience sample of undergraduates, we added some rudimentary information about redistributive effects to each of these programs (for example, "the most benefits would go to those who own the most expensive homes," or "the most benefits would go to those who save the most for retirement"). In these program frames where respondents learned that the owners of expensive homes would get more tax subsidies, support for the tax expenditure delivery mechanism dropped somewhat, but support for the direct spending programs plummeted when respondents were told that the owners of expensive homes would get larger checks from the federal government. Though we cannot generalize from this sample, it provides suggestive evidence that citizens are more willing to support a tax expenditure program that provides benefits to the already-wealthy than a direct payment program that does the same thing.

20. Regression models including delivery mechanism alongside several other standard predictors of social spending preferences show that the impact of delivery mechanism on preferences is also substantive when compared to other standard predictors of government spending views: the standardized impact of delivery mechanism on support for the mortgage interest and retirement savings programs, for example, was roughly half that of political ideology.

21. See, for example, Gilens 1999; Petersen 2012.

22. Friedman and Friedman 1990.

23. Page and Jacobs 2009.

24. Franklin and Jackson 1993; Ura and Ellis 2012.

25. Hinich and Munger 1996.

26. See, for example, Feldman and Zaller 1992.

27. Conover and Feldman 1981; Ellis and Stimson 2012.

28. Pew Research Center 2019.

29. Hetherington 2005, 12.

30. Rudolph and Evans 2005, 661.

31. Hetherington 2005.

32. Ellis and Stimson 2012.

33. Hetherington and Rudolph 2015, chap. 7. At the aggregate level, however, what this means is that it is likely to be very difficult to generate support for government intervention to solve social problems in an era when trust in government is low. This is particularly true in an environment that is heavily polarized along partisan lines, where bipartisan agreement on major social policy areas is exceedingly rare (Abramowitz 2010; Campbell 2018) and partisans are very unlikely to trust the "other side" to govern effectively. Government gridlock, in other words, is at least in part a function of declining political trust and the spread of a belief that any activity conducted by "the federal government" is likely to be inefficient, ineffective, and corrupt (see Hetherington and Rudolph 2015, chap. 10).

34. Rudolph and Evans 2005; see also Rudolph 2009.
35. The remaining respondents, who said that they trusted the government "only some of the time" are excluded from these charts. The effects of spending frame for these respondents generally fall in between the other two groups.
36. Zellner 1962. Because the equations for each of the two subgroups within each policy area are being estimated using the same time frame and the same set of independent variables, this method allows for the errors of the equations (for example, other factors left out of the model that may affect program support in both frames) to be correlated with one another.
37. Rudolph 2009.
38. In models that do not segment respondents by ideology, ideology is a stronger predictor of program support for the four direct spending programs than it is for the four tax expenditure programs, again showing that direct spending programs are viewed more strongly through an ideological lens.
39. Howard 1997; see also Mettler 2011.
40. Page and Jacobs 2009; Ellis and Stimson 2012.

Chapter 5: Deservingness, Race, and Social Spending

1. Grogger and Karoly 2009.
2. For comprehensive overviews of the political evolution of the EITC, see Hoffman and Seidman 2003; Holt 2006.
3. Grogger 2003.
4. See, for example, Feldman and Zaller 1992; Ellis and Stimson 2012; Hetherington 2005; Jacoby 1994; Rudolph and Evans 2005.
5. See, for example, Aarøe and Petersen 2014; Slothuus 2007; van Oorschot 2006.
6. Cox 2001; Green-Pedersen 2001; Slothuus 2007.
7. See, for example, Petersen 2012.
8. Cosmides and Tooby 2005.
9. Sugiyama, Tooby, and Cosmides 2002; van Oorschot 2006.
10. Petersen 2012.
11. Katz 1990.
12. See, for example, Kluegel and Smith 1986.
13. Van Oorschot 2000; see also Kallio and Kouvo 2014; Larsen 2006.
14. On American values and views of human nature, see Barker and Carman 2000.
15. Hochschild 1981; van Oorschot and Halman 2000.
16. Petersen et al. 2010; Petersen 2012.
17. Jost 2009.
18. Skitka et al. 2002.
19. Van Oorschot 2006.
20. Schneider and Ingram 1993, 334.
21. Schneider and Ingram 1993; see also Schneider and Sidney 2009.
22. Schneider and Ingram 1993.
23. See Link and Oldendick 1996; Schroedel and Jordan 1998.

24. Bobo 1998; DeSante 2013.

25. Sniderman and Piazza 1995.

26. Gilens 1996; Kellstedt 2003.

27. Gilens 1999, 67.

28. Ibid. 137.

29. See, for example, Hedegaard 2014; Petersen et al. 2010.

30. Ellis and Stimson 2012.

31. On mass opinion, see, for example, Zaller 1992.

32. Faricy and Ellis 2014; Haselswerdt and Bartels 2015.

33. Schneider and Ingram 1993; Ellis and Stimson 2012.

34. Williamson 2017.

35. On perceptions of those who are not working, see Applebaum 2001; on views of the wealthy, see McCall 2013.

36. See, for example, Cantril and Cantril 1999.

37. See, for example, Jacoby 2000.

38. Gilens 1999; see also Iyengar 1990; Will 1993; Hancock 2004. When it comes to tax expenditures, many citizens fail to recognize or characterize benefits delivered through the tax code as specific forms of government intervention in the economy (see, for example, Mettler 2011). These perceptions are often reinforced by how messages are framed by policymakers, who tend to categorize welfare, but not tax expenditures, as an archetypal form of "government spending." In fact, policymakers often describe the expansion of tax expenditure programs as facilitating a reduction in the size and reach of government (Howard 1997).

39. Feldman and Zaller 1992; Hetherington 2005; Hetherington and Rudolph 2015; Hochschild 1981; McCall 2013.

40. Stimson 2016.

41. Ellis and Faricy 2011.

42. Aarøe and Petersen 2014.

43. The order in which respondents received each of these three vignettes was also randomized.

44. The egalitarianism scale was created by combining levels of agreement with three statements: "One of the biggest problems in this country is that we don't give everyone an equal chance"; "incomes should be more equal because every family's need for food, housing, and so on, is the same"; and "this country would be better off if we worried less about how equal people are."

45. Jost 2011.

46. Hasenfeld and Raferty 1989.

47. Gilens 1999.

48. We restrict our analyses here and in what follows to nonblack respondents only.

49. Respondents were asked specifically about their support for welfare spending at the state level; while more accurate for the purposes of understanding how welfare monies are allocated, this question was a bit of a departure from more conventional wordings asking respondents simply for their views on "welfare." It is worth noting that the

magnitude of the coefficients in the analyses to follow mirror closely what is seen using similar predictors with the 2012 American National Election Study (which, again, asks more simply about support for "welfare" spending). The ANES does not ask about support for the EITC, however, so we cannot compare results for welfare spending in that survey to comparable attitudes for the EITC.

50. Henry and Sears 2002; see also Kinder and Sears 1981.
51. This 2014 CCES module also asked respondents about explicit prejudices toward whites and blacks by using a version of the ANES "work ethic" scale, which asks respondents to rate the work ethic of citizens of various racial groups on a 1–7 scale ranging from "lazy" to "hardworking." This measure of racial prejudice has been used in past work (see, for example, Gilens 1998; Hutchings 2009; Krupnikov and Piston 2015) as an alternative to the conventional symbolic racism scale. We have replicated the results in table 5.5, substituting a measure of racial prejudice (see Piston 2018) derived from these questions (responses to the "white" work ethic scale–responses to the "black" work ethic scale), and the results are nearly identical to what is presented in table 5.5. This measure is not available for our subsequent studies, but it at least provides some confidence that the results here are not a function of the use of the particular scale of prejudice that we employ.
52. In addition, we see in this model that a respondent's level of trust in government is significantly predictive of attitudes toward welfare spending, but not attitudes toward the EITC. This finding reinforces the findings regarding the impact of trust shown in chapter 4.
53. Gilens 1999.

Chapter 6: The Public and the Private Welfare State

1. Katz 1990.
2. Williamson 2017.
3. Thornton 2019.
4. Bellafiore 2018.
5. Gale et al. 2019.
6. Tax Policy Center 2020.
7. For an extended discussion of this point, see Block and Manza 1997.
8. Sides, Tesler, and Vavreck 2018.
9. Marr et al. 2016.
10. Internal Revenue Service 2019.
11. Faricy 2015.
12. On class bias in American policymaking, see Bartels 2016; Gilens 2011; Branham, Soroka, and Wlezien 2017.
13. Enns 2015; Soroka and Wlezien 2010.
14. Jardina 2019.
15. Faricy 2015.
16. Hetherington and Rudolph 2015.
17. NPR Staff 2011.

REFERENCES

Aarøe, Lene, and Michael Bang Petersen. 2014. "Crowding Out Culture: Scandinavians and Americans Agree on Social Welfare in the Face of Deservingness Cues." *Journal of Politics* 76(3): 684–97.

Abramowitz, Alan I. 2010. *The Disappearing Center: Engaged Citizens, Polarization, and American Democracy.* New Haven, Conn.: Yale University Press.

Achen, Christopher H., and Larry M. Bartels. 2016. *Democracy for Realists: Why Elections Do Not Produce Responsive Government.* Princeton, N.J.: Princeton University Press.

Achterberg, Peter, Dick Houtman, and Anton Derks. 2011. "Two of a Kind? An Empirical Investigation of Anti-welfarism and Economic Egalitarianism." *Public Opinion Quarterly* 75(4): 748–60.

Ahearn, William. 2007. "Chairman Rangel Calls Popular Tax Breaks Untouchable, but He's Not So Afraid of Them." Washington, D.C.: Tax Foundation (November 14). https://taxfoundation.org/chairman-rangel-calls-popular-tax-breaks-untouchable-hes-not-so-afraid-them/.

Alesina, Alberto, and Edward Glaeser. 2004. *Fighting Poverty in the U.S. and Europe: A World of Difference.* Oxford: Oxford University Press.

Applebaum, Lauren D. 2001. "The Influence of Perceived Deservingness on Policy Decisions Regarding Aid to the Poor." *Political Psychology* 22(3): 419–42.

Ashok, Vivelinn L., and Gregory A. Huber. 2019. "Do Means of Program Delivery and Distributional Consequences Affect Policy Support? Experimental Evidence About the Sources of Citizens' Policy Opinions." *Political Behavior*, 1–22. https://doi.org/10.1007/s11109-019-09534-z.

Barker, David C., and Christopher Jan Carman. 2000. "The Spirit of Capitalism? Religious Doctrine, Values, and Economic Attitude Constructs." *Political Behavior* 22(1): 1–27.

Bartels, Larry M. 2016. *Unequal Democracy: The Political Economy of the New Gilded Age*, 2nd ed. Princeton, N.J.: Princeton University Press.

Bellafiore, Robert. 2018. "Tax Expenditures Before and After the Tax Cuts and Jobs Act." *Fiscal Fact* 627. Washington, D.C.: Tax Foundation (December). https://files.taxfoundation.org/20190313114537/Tax-Foundation-FF627.pdf.

Block, Fred, and Jeff Manza. 1997. "Could We End Poverty in a Postindustrial Society? The Case for a Progressive Negative Income Tax." *Politics and Society* 25(4): 473–511.

Bobo, Lawrence. 1998. "Race, Interests, and Beliefs About Affirmative Action: Unanswered Questions and New Directions." *American Behavioral Scientist* 41(7): 985–1003.

Branham, J. Alexander, Stuart N. Soroka, and Christopher Wlezien. 2017. "When Do the Rich Win?" *Political Science Quarterly* 132(1): 43–62.

Brooks, Clem, and Jeff Manza. 2008. *Why Welfare States Persist: The Importance of Public Opinion in Democracies.* Chicago: University of Chicago Press.

———. 2013. "A Broken Public? Americans' Responses to the Great Recession." *American Sociological Review* 78(5): 727–48.

Burman, Leonard E., Christopher Geissler, and Eric J. Toder. 2008. "How Big Are Total Individual Income Tax Expenditures, and Who Benefits from Them?" *American Economic Review* 98(2): 79–83.

Busemeyer, Marius R. 2009. "Social Democrats and the New Partisan Politics of Public Investment in Education." *Journal of European Public Policy* 16(1): 107–26.

Campbell, James E. 2018. *Polarized: Making Sense of a Divided America.* Princeton, N.J.: Princeton University Press.

Cantril, Albert H., and Susan Davis Cantril. 1999. *Reading Mixed Signals: Ambivalence in Public Opinion About Government.* Washington, D.C.: Woodrow Wilson Press.

Carsey, Thomas M., and Geoffrey C. Layman. 2006. "Changing Sides or Changing Minds? Party Identification and Policy Preferences in the American Electorate." *American Journal of Political Science* 50(2): 464–77.

Chait, Jonathan. 2011. "The Triumph of Taxophobia." *Democracy: A Journal of Ideas* 20(Spring). https://democracyjournal.org/magazine/20/the-triumph-of-taxophobia/.

Claassen, Christopher, Patrick Tucker, and Steven S. Smith. 2015. "Ideological Labels in America." *Political Behavior* 37(2): 253–78.

Claggett, William J. M., and Bryon E. Shafer. 2010. *The American Public Mind: The Issues Structure of Mass Politics in the Postwar United States.* Cambridge: Cambridge University Press.

Condon, Meghan, and Amber Wichowsky. 2020. "Inequality in the Social Mind: Social Comparison and Support for Redistribution." *Journal of Politics* 82(1): 149–61.

Congressional Budget Office. 2013. "The Distribution of Major Tax Expenditures in the Individual Tax System." Washington: CBO (May 29). https://www.cbo.gov/publication/43768.

———. 2016. "Monthly Budget Review: Summary for Fiscal Year 2016." Washington: CBO (November 7). https://www.cbo.gov/publication/52152.

Conover, Pamela Johnston, and Stanley Feldman. 1981. "The Origins and Meaning of Liberal/Conservative Self-identifications." *American Journal of Political Science* 25(4): 617–45.

Converse, Philip E. 1964. "The Nature of Belief Systems in Mass Publics." *Critical Review* 18(1): 1–74.

Cosmides, Leda, and John Tooby. 2005. "Neurocognitive Adaptations Designed for Social Exchange." In *The Handbook of Evolutionary Psychology*, edited by David M. Buss. Hoboken, N.J.: John Wiley & Sons.

Cox, Robert Henry. 2001. "The Social Construction of an Imperative: Why Welfare Reform Happened in Denmark and the Netherlands but Not in Germany." *World Politics* 53(3): 463–98.

Dalton, Russell J. 2015. *The Good Citizen: How a Younger Generation Is Reshaping American Politics*. Washington, D.C.: Congressional Quarterly Press.

Delli Carpini, Michael X., and Scott Keeter. 1996. *What Americans Know About Politics and Why It Matters*. New Haven, Conn.: Yale University Press.

Department of Housing and Urban Development. 2018. *Fiscal Year 2018 Budget*. https://www.hud.gov/sites/documents/FY_18_CJS_COMBINED.PDF.

DeSante, Christopher D. 2013. "Working Twice as Hard to Get Half as Far: Race, Work Ethic, and America's Deserving Poor." *American Journal of Political Science* 57(2): 342–56.

Eastman, Scott, and Anna Tyger. 2019. "The Home Mortgage Interest Deduction." *Fiscal Fact* 671. Washington, D.C.: Tax Foundation (October). https://taxfoundation.org/home-mortgage-interest-deduction/.

Egan, Patrick J. 2013. *Partisan Priorities: How Issue Ownership Drives and Distorts American Politics*. Cambridge: Cambridge University Press.

Eismeier, Theodore J. 1982. "Public Preferences About Government Spending: Partisan, Social, and Attitudinal Sources of Policy Differences." *Political Behavior* 4(2): 133–45.

Ellis, Christopher. 2017. *Putting Inequality in Context: Class, Public Opinion, and Representation in the United States*. Ann Arbor: University of Michigan Press.

Ellis, Christopher, and Christopher Faricy. 2011. "Social Policy and Public Opinion: How the Ideological Direction of Spending Influences Public Mood." *Journal of Politics* 73(4): 1095–1110.

Ellis, Christopher, and James A. Stimson. 2012. *Ideology in America*. Cambridge: Cambridge University Press.

Employee Benefit Research Institute. 2016. *The EBRI Databook on Employee Benefits*. Washington, D.C.: EBRI.

Enns, Peter K. 2015. "Relative Policy Support and Coincidental Representation." *Perspectives on Politics* 13(4): 1053–64.

Enns, Peter, and Christopher Wlezien, eds. 2011. *Who Gets Represented?* New York: Russell Sage Foundation.

Erikson, Robert S., Michael B. MacKuen, and James A. Stimson. 2002. *The Macro Polity*. Cambridge: Cambridge University Press.

Esping-Andersen, Gøsta. 1990. *The Three Worlds of Welfare Capitalism*. Princeton, N.J.: Princeton University Press.

Faricy, Christopher. 2015. *Welfare for the Wealthy: Parties, Social Spending, and Inequality in the United States*. Cambridge: Cambridge University Press.

Faricy, Christopher, and Christopher Ellis. 2014. "Public Attitudes Toward Social Spending in the United States: The Differences Between Direct Spending and Tax Expenditures." *Political Behavior* 36(1): 53–76.

Federal Reserve. 2019. *Report on the Economic Well-being of U.S. Households in 2018.* Washington, D.C.: Board of Governors of the Federal Reserve System.

Feldman, Stanley. 1988. "Structure and Consistency in Public Opinion: The Role of Core Beliefs and Values." *American Journal of Political Science* 32(2): 416–40.

Feldman, Stanley, and Marco R. Steenbergen. 2001. "The Humanitarian Foundation of Public Support for Social Welfare." *American Journal of Political Science* 45(3): 658–77.

Feldman, Stanley, and John Zaller. 1992. "The Political Culture of Ambivalence: Ideological Responses to the Welfare State." *American Journal of Political Science* 36(1): 268–307.

Fong, Christina. 2001. "Social Preferences, Self-interest, and the Demand for Distribution." *Journal of Public Economics* 82(2): 225–46.

Franklin, Charles H., and John E. Jackson. 1993. "The Dynamics of Party Identification." *American Political Science Review* 77(4): 957–73.

Free, Lloyd A., and Hadley Cantril. 1969. *The Political Beliefs of Americans: A Study of Public Opinion.* New Brunswick, N.J.: Rutgers University Press.

Friedman, Milton, and Rose Friedman. 1990. *Free to Choose: A Personal Statement.* New York: Houghton Mifflin Harcourt.

Funk, Carolyn L. 2000. "The Dual Influence of Self-interest and Societal Interest in Public Opinion." *Political Research Quarterly* 53(1): 37–62.

Gale, William G., Hilary Gelfond, Aaron Krupkin, Mark Mazur, and Eric Toder. 2019. "Effects of the Tax Cuts and Jobs Act: A Preliminary Analysis." *National Tax Journal* 71(4): 589–612.

Gilens, Martin. 1996. "Race and Poverty in America: Public Misperceptions and the American News Media." *Public Opinion Quarterly* 60(4): 515–41.

———. 1998. "Racial Attitudes and Race-Neutral Social Policies: White Opposition to Welfare and the Politics of Racial Inequality." In *Perception and Prejudice: Race and Politics in the United States*, edited by Jon Hurwitz and Mark Peffley. New Haven, Conn.: Yale University Press.

———. 1999. *Why Americans Hate Welfare: Race, Media, and the Politics of Antipoverty Policy.* Chicago: University of Chicago Press.

———. 2011. "Policy Consequences of Representational Inequality." In *Who Gets Represented?*, edited by Peter K. Enns and Christopher Wlezien. New York: Russell Sage Foundation.

Goren, Paul. (2008). "The Two Faces of Government Spending." *Political Research Quarterly* 61(1): 147–57.

Gottschalk, Peter, and Sheldon Danziger. 2005. "Inequality of Wage Rates, Earnings, and Family Income in the United States, 1975–2002." *Review of Income and Wealth* 51(2): 231–54.

Green-Pedersen, Christoffer. 2001. "Welfare State Retrenchment in Denmark and the Netherlands, 1982–1998: The Role of Party Competition and Party Consensus." *Comparative Political Studies* 34(9): 963–85.

Grogger, Jeffrey. 2003. "The Effects of Time Limits, the EITC, and Other Policy Changes on Welfare Use, Work, and Income Among Female-Headed Families." *Review of Economics and Statistics* 85(2): 394–408.

Grogger, Jeffrey, and Lynn A. Karoly. 2009. *Welfare Reform: Effects of a Decade of Change.* Cambridge, Mass.: Harvard University Press.

Grossmann, Matt, and David A. Hopkins. 2016. *Asymmetric Politics: Ideological Republicans and Group Interest Democrats.* Oxford: Oxford University Press.

Hacker, Jacob S. 2002. *The Divided Welfare State: The Battle over Public and Private Social Benefits in the United States.* Cambridge: Cambridge University Press.

Hacker, Jacob S., Philipp Rehm, and Mark Schlesinger. 2013. "The Insecure American: Economic Experiences, Financial Worries, and Policy Attitudes." *Perspectives on Politics* 11(1): 23–49.

Hancock, Ange-Marie. 2004. *The Politics of Disgust: The Public Identity of the Welfare Queen.* New York: New York University Press.

Hansen, John Mark. 1998. "Individuals, Institutions, and Public Preferences over Public Finance." *American Political Science Review* 92(3): 513–31.

Haselswerdt, Jake, and Brandon L. Bartels. 2015. "Public Opinion, Policy Tools, and the Status Quo: Evidence from a Survey Experiment." *Political Research Quarterly* 68(3): 607–21.

Hasenfeld, Yeheskel, and Jane A. Rafferty. 1989. "The Determinants of Public Attitudes Toward the Welfare State." *Social Forces* 67(4): 1027–48.

Hedegaard, Troels Fage. 2014. "The Policy Design Effect: Proximity as a Micro-level Explanation of the Effect of Policy Designs on Social Benefit Attitudes." *Scandinavian Political Studies* 37(4): 366–84.

Henderson, Michael, and D. Sunshine Hillygus. 2011. "The Dynamics of Health Care Opinion, 2008–2010: Partisanship, Self-interest, and Racial Resentment." *Journal of Health Politics, Policy, and Law* 36(6): 945–60.

Henderson, Tammy L., Pamela A. Monroe, James C. Garand, and Diane C. Burts. 1995. "Explaining Public Opinion Toward Government Spending on Child Care." *Family Relations* 44(1): 37–45.

Henry, P. J., and David O. Sears. 2002. "The Symbolic Racism 2000 Scale." *Political Psychology* 23(2): 253–83.

Hetherington, Marc J. 2005. *Why Trust Matters: Declining Political Trust and the Demise of American Liberalism.* Princeton, N.J.: Princeton University Press.

Hetherington, Marc J., and Thomas J. Rudolph. 2015. *Why Washington Won't Work: Polarization, Political Trust, and the Governing Crisis.* Chicago: University of Chicago Press.

Hinich, Melvin J., and Michael C. Munger. 1996. *Ideology and the Theory of Political Choice.* Ann Arbor: University of Michigan Press.

Hochschild, Jennifer L. 1981. *What's Fair? American Beliefs About Distributive Justice.* Cambridge, Mass.: Harvard University Press.

Hoffman, Saul D., and Laurence S. Seidman. 2003. *Helping Working Families: The Earned Income Tax Credit.* Kalamazoo, Mich.: Upjohn Institute.

Holt, Steve. 2006. "The Earned Income Tax Credit at Age 30: What We Know." Washington, D.C.: Brookings Institution (February).

Howard, Christopher. 1997. *The Hidden Welfare State: Tax Expenditures and Social Policy in the United States*. Princeton, N.J.: Princeton University Press.

Hutchings, Vincent L. 2009. "Change or More of the Same? Evaluating Racial Attitudes in the Obama Era." *Public Opinion Quarterly* 73(5): 917–42.

Internal Revenue Service. 2019. "EITC Participation Rate by State." https://www.eitc.irs.gov /eitc-central/participation-rate/eitc-participation-rate-by-states (last updated October 8, 2019).

Iyengar, Shanto. 1990. "Framing Responsibility for Political Issues: The Case of Poverty." *Political Behavior* 12(1): 19–40.

Iyengar, Shanto, and Sean J. Westwood. 2015. "Fear and Loathing Across Party Lines: New Evidence on Group Polarization." *American Journal of Political Science* 59(3): 690–707.

Jacoby, William G. 1994. "Public Attitudes Toward Government Spending." *American Journal of Political Science* 38(2): 336–61.

———. 2000. "Issue Framing and Public Opinion on Government Spending." *American Journal of Political Science* 44(4): 750–67.

———. 2006. "Value Choices and American Public Opinion." *American Journal of Political Science* 50(3): 706–23.

Jardina, Ashley. 2019. *White Identity Politics*. Cambridge: Cambridge University Press.

Johnston, Christopher D., Howard G. Lavine, and Christopher M. Federico. 2017. *Open Versus Closed: Personality, Identity, and the Politics of Redistribution*. Cambridge: Cambridge University Press.

Joint Committee on Taxation. 2019. "Estimates of Federal Tax Expenditures for Fiscal Years 2019–2023." Report JCX-55-19. Washington: U.S. Government Printing Office (December 18).

Jost, John T. 2009. "'Elective Affinities': On the Psychological Bases of Left-Right Differences." *Psychological Inquiry* 20(2/3): 129–41.

———. 2011. "System Justification Theory as Compliment, Complement, and Corrective to Theories of Social Identification and Social Dominance." In *Social Motivation*, edited by David Dunning. Frontiers of Social Psychology. New York: Psychology Press.

Kaiser Family Foundation. 2019. "Medicaid State Fact Sheets." May 27. https://www.kff .org/interactive/medicaid-state-fact-sheets/ (accessed September 22, 2020).

Kallio, Johanna, and Antti Kouvo. 2014. "Street-Level Bureaucrats and the General Public's Deservingness Perceptions of Social Assistance Recipients in Finland." *Social Policy and Administration* 49(3): 316–34.

Katz, Michael B. 1990. *The Undeserving Poor: From the War on Poverty to the War on Welfare*. New York: Pantheon.

Kellstedt, Paul M. 2003. *The Mass Media and the Dynamics of American Racial Attitudes*. Cambridge: Cambridge University Press.

Kelly, Nathan J. 2020. *America's Inequality Trap*. Chicago: University of Chicago Press.

Kelly, Nathan J., and Peter K. Enns. 2010. "Inequality and the Dynamics of Public Opinion: The Self-Reinforcing Link Between Economic Inequality and Mass Preferences." *American Journal of Political Science* 54(4): 855–70.

Key, V. O. 1961. *Public Opinion and American Democracy*. New York: Alfred A. Knopf.

Kiel, Paul, and Jesse Eisinger. 2018. "How the IRS Was Gutted." *ProPublica*, December 11. https://www.propublica.org/article/how-the-irs-was-gutted/.

Kinder, Donald R., and David O. Sears. 1981. "Prejudice and Politics: Symbolic Racism Versus Racial Threats to the Good Life." *Journal of Personality and Social Psychology* 40(3): 414–31.

Kluegel, James R., and Eliot R. Smith. 1986. *Beliefs About Inequality: Americans' Views of What Is and What Ought to Be.* New York: Routledge.

Krupnikov, Yanna, and Spencer Piston. 2015. "Accentuating the Negative: Candidate Race and Campaign Strategy." *Political Communication* 32(1): 152–73.

Larsen, Christian Albrekt. 2006. *The Institutional Logic of Welfare Attitudes: How Welfare Regimes Influence Public Support.* Hampshire: Ashgate Publishing.

Lazarus, Jeffrey, and Shauna Reilly. 2010. "The Electoral Benefits of Distributive Spending." *Political Research Quarterly* 63(2): 343–55.

Levitt, Steven D., and James M. Snyder Jr. 1997. "The Impact of Federal Spending on House Election Outcomes." *Journal of Political Economy* 105(1): 30–54.

Link, Michael W., and Robert W. Oldendick. 1996. "Social Construction and White Attitudes Toward Equal Opportunity and Multiculturalism." *Journal of Politics* 58(1): 149–68.

Marr, Chuck, Chye-Ching Huang, Cecile Murray, and Arloc Sherman. 2016. "Strengthening the EITC for Childless Workers Would Promote Work and Reduce Poverty." Washington, D.C.: Center on Budget and Policy Priorities (April 11). https://www.cbpp.org /research/federal-tax/strengthening-the-eitc-for-childless-workers-would-promote-work -and-reduce.

Mason, Lilliana. 2018. *Uncivil Agreement: How Politics Became Our Identity.* Chicago: University of Chicago Press.

Mayhew, David R. 1974. *Congress: The Electoral Connection.* New Haven, Conn.: Yale University Press.

McCall, Leslie. 2013. *The Undeserving Rich: American Beliefs About Inequality, Opportunity, and Redistribution.* Cambridge: Cambridge University Press.

McCall, Leslie, and Lane Kenworthy. 2009. "Americans' Social Policy Preferences in the Era of Rising Inequality." *Perspectives on Politics* 7(3): 459–84.

McClelland, Robert, and Nikhita Airi. 2020. "Effective Income Tax Rates Have Fallen for the Top One Percent Since World War II." Washington, D.C.: Tax Policy Center (January 6). https://www.taxpolicycenter.org/taxvox/effective-income-tax-rates-have -fallen-top-one-percent-world-war-ii.

McClosky, Herbert, and John Zaller. 1984. *The American Ethos: Public Attitudes Toward Democracy and Capitalism.* Cambridge, Mass.: Harvard University Press.

Mettler, Suzanne. 2010. "Reconstituting the Submerged State: The Challenges of Social Policy Reform in the Obama Era." *Perspectives on Politics* 8(3): 803–24.

———. 2011. *The Submerged State: How Invisible Government Policies Undermine American Democracy.* Chicago: University of Chicago Press.

Mettler, Suzanne, and Jeffrey M. Stonecash. 2008. "Government Program Usage and Political Voice." *Social Science Quarterly* 89(2): 273–93.

Mondak, Jeffery J. 1993. "Public Opinion and Heuristic Processing of Source Cues." *Political Behavior* 15(2): 167–92.

Morgan, Kimberly J., and Andrea Louise Campbell. 2011. *The Delegated Welfare State: Medicare, Markets, and the Governance of Social Policy.* Oxford: Oxford University Press.

NPR Staff. 2011. "President Obama's Speech on Deficit Cutting." NPR, April 13. http://www.npr.org/2011/04/13/135383045/.

Office of Management and Budget. 2019. *Budget of the U.S. Government, Fiscal Year 2019.* Washington: OMB.

Organization for Economic Cooperation and Development. 2010. *Tax Expenditures in OECD Countries.* Paris: OECD.

———. 2020. "Social Expenditure Database." https://www.oecd.org/social/expenditure.htm.

Page, Benjamin I., and Lawrence R. Jacobs. 2009. *Class War? What Americans Really Think About Economic Inequality.* Chicago: University of Chicago Press.

Petersen, Michael Bang. 2012. "Social Welfare as Small-Scale Help: Evolutionary Psychology and the Deservingness Heuristic." *American Journal of Political Science* 56(1): 1–16.

Petersen, Michael B., Rune Slothuus, Rune Stubager, and Lise Togeby. 2010. "Deservingness Versus Values in Public Opinion on Welfare: The Automaticity of the Deservingness Heuristic." *European Journal of Political Research* 50(1): 24–52.

Pew Research Center. 2019. "Public Trust in Government, 1958–2019." Washington, D.C.: Pew Research Center (April 11). https://www.people-press.org/2019/04/11/public-trust-in-government-1958-2019/.

Pierson, Paul. 1994. *Dismantling the Welfare State? Reagan, Thatcher, and the Politics of Retrenchment.* Cambridge: Cambridge University Press.

Piketty, Thomas. 2014. *Capitalism in the Twenty-First Century.* Cambridge, Mass.: Harvard University Press.

Piston, Spencer. 2018. *Class Attitudes in America: Sympathy for the Poor, Resentment of the Rich, and Political Implications.* Cambridge: Cambridge University Press.

Popp, Elizabeth, and Thomas J. Rudolph. 2011. "A Tale of Two Ideologies: Explaining Public Support for Economic Interventions." *Journal of Politics* 73(3): 808–20.

Prasad, Monica. 2018. *Starving the Beast: Ronald Reagan and the Tax Cut Revolution.* New York: Russell Sage Foundation.

Reno, Virginia, and Elisa Walker. 2019. "Social Security Benefits, Finances, and Policy Options: A Primer." Washington, D.C.: National Academy of Social Insurance (July). https://www.nasi.org/sites/default/files/research/NASI%20Social%20Security%20Primer%202011.pdf.

Rokeach, Milton. 1973. *The Nature of Human Values.* New York: Free Press.

Rubin, Richard, and Margaret Collins. 2014. "Early Tap of 401(k) Replaces Homes as American Piggy Bank." *Bloomberg,* May 6. https://www.bloomberg.com/news/articles/2014-05-06/early-tap-of-401-k-replaces-homes-as-american-piggy-bank.

Rubin, Robert E. 2012. "The Fiscal Delusion." *New York Times,* November 12. https://www.nytimes.com/2012/11/13/opinion/rubin-deluding-ourselves-over-the-fiscal-cliff.html.

Rudolph, Thomas J. 2009. "Political Trust, Ideology, and Public Support for Tax Cuts." *Public Opinion Quarterly* 73(1): 144–58.

Rudolph, Thomas J., and Jillian Evans. 2005. "Political Trust, Ideology, and Public Support for Government Spending." *American Journal of Political Science* 49(3): 660–71.

Salamon, Lester M., ed. 1989. *Beyond Privatization: The Tools of Government Action.* Washington, D.C.: Urban Institute Press.

Schneider, Anne, and Helen Ingram. 1993. "Social Construction of Target Populations: Implications for Politics and Policy." *American Political Science Review* 87(2): 334–47.

Schneider, Anne, and Mara Sidney. 2009. "What Is Next for Policy Design and Social Construction Theory?" *Policy Studies Journal* 37(1): 103–19.

Schroedel, Jean Reith, and Daniel R. Jordan. 1998. "Senate Voting and Social Construction of Target Populations: A Study of AIDS Policy Making, 1987–1992." *Journal of Health Politics, Policy, and Law* 23(1): 107–32.

Sears, David O., and Jack Citrin. 1985. *Tax Revolt: Something for Nothing in California,* enlarged ed. Cambridge, Mass.: Harvard University Press.

Sides, John, Michael Tesler, and Lynn Vavreck. 2018. *Identity Crisis: The 2016 Presidential Campaign and the Battle for the Meaning of America.* Princeton, N.J.: Princeton University Press.

Silver, Jasmine R., and Justin T. Pickett. 2015. "Toward a Better Understanding of Politicized Policing Attitudes: Conflicted Conservatism and Support for Police Use of Force." *Criminology* 53(4): 650–76.

Skitka, Linda J., Elizabeth Mullen, Thomas Griffin, Susan Hutchinson, and Brian Chamberlin. 2002. "Dispositions, Scripts, or Motivated Correction? Understanding Ideological Differences in Explanations for Social Problems." *Journal of Personality and Social Psychology* 83(2): 470–87.

Slothuus, Rune. 2007. "Framing Deservingness to Win Support for Welfare State Retrenchment." *Scandinavian Political Studies* 30(3): 323–44.

Sniderman, Paul M., and Thomas L. Piazza. 1995. *The Scar of Race.* Cambridge, Mass.: Harvard University Press.

Social Security Administration. 2017. *The 2017 Annual Report of the Board of Trustees of the Federal Old-Age and Survivors Insurance and Federal Disability Insurance Trust Funds.* Washington: U.S. Government Printing Office. https://www.ssa.gov/OACT /TR/2017/tr2017.pdf.

Soroka, Stuart N., and Christopher Wlezien. 2010. *Degrees of Democracy: Politics, Public Opinion, and Policy.* Cambridge: Cambridge University Press.

Stein, Robert M., and Kenneth N. Bickers. 1997. *Perpetuating the Pork Barrel: Policy Subsystems and American Democracy.* Cambridge: Cambridge University Press.

Stimson, James A. 2016. *Tides of Consent: How Public Opinion Shapes American Politics.* Cambridge: Cambridge University Press.

Stuerle, C. Eugene. 2000. "Summers on Social Tax Expenditures." Washington, D.C.: Urban Institute (December 11). https://www.urban.org/research/publication/summers -social-tax-expenditures-part-1-2/view/full_report.

Sugiyama, L. S., John Tooby, and Leda Cosmides. 2002. "Cross-cultural Evidence of Cognitive Adaptations for Social Exchange Among the Shiwiar of Ecuadorian Amazonia." *Proceedings of the National Academy of Sciences* 99(17): 11537–42.

Surrey, Stanley S. 1974. *Pathways to Tax Reform: The Concept of Tax Expenditures.* Cambridge, Mass.: Harvard University Press.

Svallfors, Stefan. 2013. "Government Quality, Egalitarianism, and Attitudes to Taxes and Social Spending: A European Comparison." *European Political Science Review* 5(3): 363–80.

Tax Policy Center. 2020. "Analysis of the Tax Cuts and Jobs Act." https://www.taxpolicy center.org/feature/analysis-tax-cuts-and-jobs-act (last updated May 8, 2020).

Teles, Steven M. 2007. "Conservative Mobilization Against Entrenched Liberalism." In *The Transformation of American Politics: Activist Government and the Rise of Conservatism*, edited by Paul Pierson and Theda Skocpol. Princeton, N.J.: Princeton University Press.

Telford, Taylor. 2019. "Income Inequality in America Is the Highest It's Been Since Census Bureau Started Tracking It, Data Shows." *Washington Post*, September 26. https://www.washingtonpost.com/business/2019/09/26/income-inequality-america -highest-its-been-since-census-started-tracking-it-data-show/.

Thornton, Alexandra. 2019. "Opinion: Being 'Fiscally Responsible' Means Cleaning Up Wasteful Tax Expenditures." *MarketWatch*, November 5. https://www.marketwatch .com/story/being-fiscally-responsible-means-cleaning-up-wasteful-tax-expenditures -2019-11-04.

Twyman, Joe. 2008. "Getting It Right: YouGov and Online Survey Research in Britain." *Journal of Elections, Public Opinion, and Parties* 18(4): 343–54.

Ura, Joseph Daniel, and Christopher C. Ellis. 2012. "Partisan Moods: Polarization and the Dynamics of Mass Party Preferences." *Journal of Politics* 74(1): 277–91.

Van Kersbergen, Kees, and Barbara Vis. 2014. *Comparative Welfare State Politics.* Cambridge: Cambridge University Press.

Van Oorschot, Wim. 2000. "Who Should Get What, and Why? On Deservingness Criteria and the Conditionality of Solidarity Among the Public." *Policy and Politics* 28(1): 33–48.

———. 2006. "Making the Difference in Social Europe: Deservingness Perceptions Among Citizens of European Welfare States." *Journal of European Social Policy* 16(1): 23–42.

Van Oorschot, Wim, and Loek Halman. 2000. "Blame or Fate, Individual or Social?" *European Societies* 2(1): 1–28.

Will, Jeffrey A. 1993. "The Dimensions of Poverty: Public Perceptions of the Deserving Poor." *Social Science Research* 22(3): 312–32.

Williamson, Vanessa S. 2017. *Read My Lips: Why Americans Are Proud to Pay Taxes.* Princeton, N.J.: Princeton University Press.

Wlezien, Christopher. 2004. "Patterns of Representation: Dynamics of Public Preferences and Policy." *Journal of Politics* 66(1): 1–24.

Wolff, Edward N. 2013. "The Asset Price Meltdown, Rising Leverage, and the Wealth of the Middle Class." *Journal of Economic Issues* 43(2): 333–42.

Zaller, John. 1992. *The Nature and Origins of Mass Opinion.* Cambridge: Cambridge University Press.

Zellner, Arnold. 1962. "An Efficient Method of Estimating Seemingly Unrelated Regressions and Tests for Aggregation Bias." *Journal of the American Statistical Association* 57(298): 348–68.

INDEX

Boldface numbers refer to figures and tables.